THE WORDS OF JESUS IN OUR GOSPELS

The Words of Jesus in Our Gospels

*A Catholic Response
to Fundamentalism*

Stanley B. Marrow

PAULIST PRESS
NEW YORK/RAMSEY/TORONTO

Library of Congress
Catalog Card Number: 79-52105

ISBN: 0-8091-2215-4

Published by Paulist Press
Editorial Office: 1865 Broadway, New York, N. Y. 10023
Business Office: 545 Island Road, Ramsey, N. J. 07446

Printed and bound in the
United States of America

Contents

To
the memory
of my mother . . .

res est ingeniosa dare

Introduction

The unexamined life, said Socrates, is not worth living. So too might one say of the unexamined faith. This little volume is intended as an aid to the examination of one specific but fundamental tenet of the Christian faith: that the Bible is the word of God. For the sake of convenience, the object of the examination is further limited to the New Testament; and that in turn to the four Gospels.

This, of course, is not a work for experts. To those who, in any capacity, are acquainted with current biblical studies there is little here that is new. But the book is not intended for them. It is meant to be an aid for the increasing number of Christians who, amid the crises that face them and their church, find their past religious education insufficient and the present available instructions inadequate.

An ever increasing number of these Christians today find themselves before opposed and rival claims made by varying groups within the church and without. The only thing such groups have in common is their ready appeal to the Bible as the word of God and hence as authoritative and beyond question.

To provide some material for reflection on the worth and value of such a crucial claim, the book assumes there are two basic approaches to its meaning. The first is to say that the Bible is the word of God and to mean literally just that. Consequently, to such a view, the Bible enjoys not only absolute authority but also total immunity from error. Such an attitude, in other words, sees a descending order from the God who reveals his divine truth to the inspired scribe, who communicates it without error to God's people, who receive it "not as the word of men but as what it really is, the word of God" (1 Thess. 2:13).

1

The second approach, accepting the Bible to be the word of God and acknowledging its authority, reverses the order of argument. It starts with the Bible itself as we have it today and, in ascending order, proceeds from it to its human authors and thence to its divine origin. This is the approach adopted here. In place of starting with the God who reveals, it starts with the believers in that revelation. It progresses from the concrete datum of the Bible here and now and argues back to what was in the beginning.

If in the course of this exposition the first approach is characterized as "fundamentalist" it is simply for lack of a better term. If the second approach is left without a specific designation it is simply because the meaning of the available antonym, "liberal," has become too variable and too extensive to be serviceable at all. There are perhaps as many reasons for describing the approach adopted here as "liberal" as there are for calling it "anti-liberal." The designation would hence be meaningless.

Such designations, however, are not at all essential to the main argument. What is essential and has to be kept in mind throughout is that both approaches are not merely legitimate but Christian. The preference of one approach over the other is not at all the triumph of orthodoxy over heresy, of truth over error.

In arguing for the reasonableness of the second approach against the first, the author is of course arguing from his own background, education and prejudice. So too will he necessarily be read. The "we" employed in the course of the argument, far from being a distancing device, is an invitation to examine the matter from the proposed point of view, to assume this order of argument from us who believe the Bible to be the word of God to the God who revealed it. The "we" is thus used in the spirit of Isaiah's "Come now, let us reason together" (Is. 1:18).

So, in full awareness of the legitimacy of both approaches within Christianity, the argument of this book proceeds from the present text of the Bible, its preservation through the centuries, its transmission from one generation to another, and its translation into different languages (chapter 1); to the various attempts to recover the words of Jesus himself as we have them reported in our Gospels (chapter 2); and to the meaning and significance of the task undertaken by the individual authors of these Gospels (chapter 3). In doing this the argument reviews the principal methods of approach that have been used in the study of the Gospels, discussing the tools available and some of the particular problems that arise from their use.

In this sense the work can be considered an introduction to the Gospels. But, in the course of the exposition, the main concern of the argument is to be kept in mind. There are good and very useful introductions to the New Testament and to the Gospels available. What this particular one tries to do is to remind the reader of two easily forgotten facts: (1) If no two people hear any speaker exactly alike, how can anyone pretend that everybody in every age hears the word of God in the same way? (2) As in understanding the human word, so too and much more in listening to the divine is there needed a great amount of labor, often arid and always demanding, which has to be expended before we can say, "This is the word of the Lord!" We all have to journey through a long and parched wilderness before we can come to the fountain of living waters.

Nevertheless, I have tried to avoid as much of the technical vocabulary as possible. This was done for the sake of maintaining the simplicity of the basic argument and preserving some clarity in its exposition. I have also tried to keep in mind that this is a work intended for the educated Christian without a sophisticated background in biblical studies. But whenever it was no longer possible to avoid certain technical terms I have tried to explain their meaning briefly, convinced that they are both necessary for the development of the argument and should be today part of the vocabulary of the educated reader.

In the effort to preserve a measure of simplicity and clarity I have also avoided identifying modern authors or works that have contributed so much to our present understanding of the New Testament. The extent of my own indebtednesss to these authors and works must be more than evident to anyone actively engaged in biblical scholarship at any level. For the reader who might wish to pursue some point or to ascertain the provenance of an opinion a brief bibliography is provided at the end.

My own indebtedness, however, extends far wider than the names of scholars or the titles of their publications. It includes my students who have helped me to understand my own position better and have compelled me to define my own presuppositions more sharply. It includes the colleague who called to my attention the need for such a book and, in his large kindness, suggested my writing it. But, more immediately, my indebtedness includes the Pontifical Biblical Institute, which made available to me the use of its excellent library, as well as those who, in their love and generosity, made a sabbatical leave in Rome so fruitful and happy.

Rome,
Pentecost Monday, 1978

1 The Word of God

There are at least two ways of understanding the phrase, "the word of God," when we apply it to our Bible. One way is that in which many of us were brought up and to which we almost always revert unconsciously. It sees God as a loving God who, as befits all lovers, speaks the mystery of his love to us. He does this first in an indirect way through the grandeur and magnificence of his creation. But, more directly, through the course of history, God communicates his revelation by means of chosen messengers, the seers and prophets of the Old Testament and the apostles and evangelists of the New.

The course of this gradually growing revelation reached its fullness in the person of Jesus Christ who, once and for all, revealed the great mystery of God's love for us. Indeed, so full a revelation of God is he that John's Gospel calls Jesus "the Word." This view of God's loving revelation is given majestic expression by the author of the Epistle to the Hebrews:

> *In many and various ways God spoke of old to our fathers by the prophets; but in these last days he has spoken to us by a Son (Heb. 1:1-2).*

In the books of the Old and the New Testaments that make up our Bible we possess the written record of this revelation through the prophets and in Jesus Christ. The Bible is read by us in our religious celebrations and proclaimed by us to be "the word of the Lord." To it many of us have grown accustomed to turn for comfort, guidance and consolation. We feel confident that we have there God's own word addressed to us individually.

The word of God in the Bible, moreover, has for us an authority

5

unmatched by any written human document, however sublime and venerable. To this word of God we turn to arbitrate disputes, to resolve moral dilemmas, and to find answers to the questions that trouble us. Recourse to the "word of God" is for us final and conclusive. In its light everything else of any moment is judged; and to its authority all human wisdom must bow.

We realize, of course, that the real picture is not quite so consistent as this. Innumerable problems arise. When we appeal to the Bible as a final authority we often find there are discordant views and opposing claims. Not only different churches have different interpretations but, very frequently, individuals within this or that community differ markedly. Christians and Christian churches take it for granted that the "word of God" is the foundation of their faith and the ultimate justification of their religious practices. The most burning issues of our day and the controversies of past ages provide us with innumerable instances of this belief in practice.

Underlying this belief is the firm conviction that in the Bible we have the accurate and inerrant record of the revelation of God to man through many centuries culminating in the revelation in Jesus Christ. We realize, of course, that no other human record can possibly make such a claim. But for us the Bible is the word of God and as such is exempt from the ordinary limitations we find in all other literary works.

Such an understanding of the "word of God" allows a whole range of variations and nuances. Almost every statement made requires further qualification. But those of us who take the phrase "the word of God" literally tend to apply it rather strictly when the need arises. Taking the phrase literally, i.e., taking the Bible to be an exact and inerrant record of the word of God to us, inevitably leads to what is called, for lack of a better word, a "fundamentalist" reading of the Bible.

The term "fundamentalist" in this context is not a judgment but a description. A "fundamentalist" method of reading the Bible is not one limited to a few sects or confined to certain regions. It is not a particularly Protestant approach to the Bible. To find the basis of the dogma of the Immaculate Conception of the Blessed Virgin in the Bible or to define papal infallibility as the expressed wish of Christ in the Gospel are alike "fundamentalist" approaches to the Bible. To look for an argument against abortion or for the ordination of women to the priesthood are equally "fundamentalist" interpretations.

But to describe the interpretation of the Bible in this way is not to say that it is correct or not, good or bad. Such a description of the approach does not decide whether or not it is possible to interpret the Bible in this way. It simply says that such a method of interpreting the Bible is "fundamentalist" because it takes for its premise the fact that the Bible is quite literally the word of God and, consequently, not subject to error.

A Possible Alternative

The "fundamentalist" method is not, however, the only way to understand our belief that the Bible is the word of God. There is at least one other way for understanding the phrase. Perhaps the best way to describe this alternative would be to look at how we came to have a Bible at all. For the sake of simplicity it would be helpful if we narrow our consideration, as far as possible, to the New Testament itself.

The "Bible" to Jesus and his followers was, of course, what we today call the Old Testament. But the Old Testament at that time was not as clearly defined a collection of books as many of us today are led to believe it to be. That is to say that, in the time of Jesus, the authoritative list of the books to be included in the Bible was not yet fixed. Such a list of the books that make up the Bible is called the canon.

In one of the books that to this day continues to be the subject of dispute between Catholics and Protestants, the former including it in their canon of Scripture and the latter rejecting it, the grandson of the author of the Book of Ecclesiasticus (Sirach) writes in the Prologue to the Greek translation of the book:

> *Whereas many great teachings have been given to us through* the law and the prophets and the others that followed them, *on account of which we should praise Israel for instruction and wisdom; and since it is necessary not only that the readers themselves should acquire understanding but also that those who love learning should be able to help*

> *the outsiders by both speaking and writing, my grandfather,*
> *after devoting himself especially to the reading of* the law
> and the prophets and the other books of our fathers, *and*
> *after acquiring considerable proficiency in them, was himself*
> *also led to write something pertaining to instruction and*
> *wisdom. . .*

The extent of that last category, "the others that followed them," "the other books of our fathers," varied greatly both within Palestine itself and outside it in the Greek-speaking Jewish communities, commonly referred to as the Diaspora. There was, however, some agreement throughout on the first two categories, "the law and the prophets." What is important for us to keep in mind is that for Jesus and his followers the Bible included at least "the law" (the Torah, as it is called in Hebrew; or the Pentateuch, as the Greeks designate the first five books of the Old Testament) and "the prophets."

At this point we do well to recall that the inclusion of books in the canon of the Old Testament was not a decision reached by the religious authorities of the day and handed down to the people. It was rather the people themselves who first came to recognize the unique authority of this book or that book for them. We can say that, in a way, the "canonization" of a given book, its inclusion among the books of the Bible, was an act of popular choice. But such a choice of course is, of its nature, neither fixed nor constant. Thus, even within Palestine itself, communities differed on what they considered to be their sacred books. The community of Qumran was inclined to include more books within its canon than did the Jerusalem community of the day. The Samaritans, on the other hand, accepted only the Torah as canonical. So, throughout the beginning of the Christian era, what was and what was not "the word of God" remained quite variable.

The Bible of the early Christian community immediately after the death of Jesus continued to be the Old Testament. But very shortly after the death and resurrection of Jesus something quite astonishing began to take place. The "words of Jesus" came to be regarded as on a par with the word of God in the Old Testament. This says a great deal more about what Christians thought and believed concerning Jesus of Nazareth than all the stories told about him in the New

Testament. That such a thing happened at all is cause for wonder; but that it took place so short a time after the death of Jesus is simply astounding.

The passage of centuries has doubtless dulled our sense of amazement at this fact. Yet an attentive reader of the Gospels cannot but be struck by the significance of this "canonization" of the words of Jesus of Nazareth. A trace, almost an illustration, of this process can be seen for example in Matthew's account of Jesus' words:

> *"You have heard that it was said to the men of old, 'You shall not kill; and whoever kills shall be liable to judgment.'* But I say to you *that every one who is angry with his brother shall be liable to judgment" (Mt. 5:21-22).*

Yet, sacred though they were to the Christians, the words of Jesus of Nazareth were not so sacred as to escape the very ordinary process of selection and modification at the hands of those who believed in him. Even the most retentive memory, if it is at all intelligent, is in fact selective. Naturally enough, not everything that Jesus said was remembered and not all that was retained was recalled in exactly the same way.

The sayings of the Lord were not listened to nor remembered as one might fixed magical formulae. The people listened to them and recalled them as the words of a loved one, a revered teacher, a great prophet. But they nevertheless listened to them as ordinary human beings listen to other human beings. They treasured the words that Jesus spoke and repeated them to others not as tape recorders do but as intelligent human beings are wont to do, exercising judgment and preference. We have no reason to believe that the audience of Jesus was any less creative or any more immune from error and misunderstanding than any other.

The Words of Jesus

An illustration of this last paragraph might help to clarify the point under discussion. Let us take the dying words of Jesus. Great and not so great men have succeeded in imposing upon the memory of mankind their parting words. One would expect that the small band of women who courageously stood by the cross when all the stalwarts had fled did manage to listen attentively and hand on faithfully the dying words of their beloved Master. Yet our Gospel accounts of the death of Jesus, full and detailed as they are, leave us bewildering alternatives: Mark's "loud cry" (Mk. 15:37), Luke's "Father, into thy hands I commit my spirit" (Lk. 23:46), and John's "It is finished" (Jn. 19:30).

Some might be inclined to argue that, except for sentimental reasons, this does not really matter very much. It is, they insist, the essential teaching of Jesus that was remembered and recalled intact and without error. Yet, in a ready-to-hand example of a saying of Jesus that is not only essential but also quite pertinent to our day, we see that this is still not the case at all.

For centuries the churches have argued for allowing divorce or for forbidding it, for permitting it in certain cases but not in others. But, whatever the position espoused, the church always appealed to the teaching of Jesus in the New Testament. So it will be good to see what the New Testament says Jesus taught about divorce.

Saint Paul, writing to the Corinthians, clearly cites the Lord's unequivocal stand against divorce:

> *To the married I give charge, not I but the Lord, that the wife should not separate from her husband . . . and that the husband should not divorce his wife (1 Cor. 7:10-11).*

Mark too echoes this categorical stand against divorce (Mk. 10:10-12). But Paul does not stop there. He goes on to add what can only be a modification of the absolute statement of Jesus. He is, however, careful to say that this is his own opinion:

> *To the rest* I say, not the Lord. . . *(1 Cor. 7:12-15).*

But it must be noted that both Paul and Mark actually modify the words of Jesus without any hint to the readers that they are doing so.

> *And he said to them, "Whoever divorces his wife and marries another, commits adultery against her; and if she divorces her husband and marries another, she commits adultery" (Mk. 10:11-12).*

Jesus had no reason to speak of a woman divorcing her husband since the Jews of his time, the people he was addressing when he spoke, did not allow a wife to divorce her husband. But both Mark and Paul, addressing non-Jewish people for whom such divorce was possible, did not hesitate to make the added clarification and put it into Jesus' mouth.

Matthew's case in this instance, however, is more illuminating still. In the Sermon on the Mount, in one of those sayings that show the words of Jesus on a par, indeed superseding, the word of the Law, we have:

> *"It was also said, 'Whoever divorces his wife, let him give her a certificate of divorce.' But I say to you that every one who divorces his wife,* except on the ground of unchastity, *makes her an adulteress; and whoever marries a divorced woman commits adultery" (Mt. 5:31-32).*

What, one can justifiably ask, did Jesus really say about divorce? He seems to have said something quite different from what the Old Testament allowed. But did the difference consist in extending the franchise to women? or was it simply a restriction of contemporary Jewish practice to the case of "unchastity"? or was it—as there is good reason to believe—an out-and-out ban on all divorce?

The recognition of the words of Jesus as equivalent to the words of Sacred Scripture did not stop Paul or Mark or Matthew from modifying them. Being the words of the Lord did not exempt the teachings of Jesus from the selectivity and the creative adaptability of human memory; nor did it preserve them from the alterations to which human usage would inevitably subject them.

The Letters of Paul

While the process of remembering and quoting the words of Jesus as Sacred Scripture was still going on, the letters of the Apostle Paul were also, in their own way, acquiring a privileged status in the Christian communities. The letters, which were addressed to various churches, must have enjoyed a wide circulation. By the end of the first century (about forty or fifty years after they were written) there must have been a collection of them known to many of the churches. The Second Epistle of Peter, written in the second century, mentions them:

> *So also our beloved brother Paul wrote to you according to*
> *the wisdom given him, speaking of this as he does* in all his
> letters. . . *(2 Pet. 3:15-16).*

Some scholars today would be inclined to see in the subsequent
words of 2 Peter evidence that the letters of Paul were not only
valued enough to be copied and collected but that they were also
regarded as "Scripture":

> *There were some things in them hard to understnad, which*
> *the ignorant and unstable twist to their own destruction, as*
> *they do* the other scriptures *(2 Pet. 3:16).*

Yet, valued and revered as they were, the letters of Paul, even
though written documents and not just uttered words, were not
exempt from the vicissitudes of popularity nor preserved from the
accidents of survival. Some letters, for instance, were evidently lost.
We possess no letter addressed to the Corinthians prior to First
Corinthians, which clearly refers to such a previous letter:

> *I wrote to you in my letter. . . (1 Cor. 5:9).*

Other, briefer letters were combined into one longer letter like
Philippians and the Second Letter to the Corinthians. Others still
were simply forged:

> *We beg you, brethren, not to be quickly shaken in mind or*
> *excited, either by spirit or by word, or* by letter purporting to
> be from us *(2 Thess. 2:2).*

Finally, as was often the case in antiquity, letters were written as
though Paul himself had written them. This was a common and not
unacceptable practice in past centuries. Most scholars today think
that the Pastoral Epistles (1 and 2 Timothy and the Epistle to Titus)
represent examples of this.

The Four Gospels

It is most likely that our Gospels were the first written documents
to come to be regarded as "Scripture" by the early Christian communities. They were, to use the technical term, part of the canon of the

Christian Bible even before the letters of Saint Paul. This admission of the Gospels into the canon, however, was not without its difficulties and obstacles. Oddly enough, the Gospel of John had a much harder time getting into the canon than did the first three Gospels. There were, of course, reasons for this; but the fact itself should make us realize that the whole process of recognizing what was and what was not to be considered the word of God was not exempted from the vicissitudes that beset human judgment and decision.

But, as in the case of the letters of Saint Paul, our Gospels were regarded as Holy Scripture long before there was any authoritative ecclesiastical pronouncement declaring them to be the "word of God." They were believed to be the word of God by the communities of believers scattered throughout the Roman Empire. It was these Christian communities that first used the Gospels as sacred books in their worship, referred to them in their instructions, and appealed to them in their debates with non-believers.

Yet here too the course was not one of smooth progress and universal harmony between the churches. The difficulty experienced by the Gospel of John has already been mentioned. To it must be added the major problem, which took centuries to settle, of a group of churches that insisted on using their one composite gospel rather than the four distinct ones of Matthew, Mark, Luke and John. There were also communities here and there that regarded other gospels than the four as sacred and authoritative.

All these problems complicated the process by which the communities of Christian believers finally came to recognize and accept certain books as the word of God to them, while ultimately rejecting many others as not altogether worthy of such honor. In other words, in the preservation and transmission of the words of Jesus himself no less than in the choice of the Gospels and the other books of the New Testament, the process of recognition that in them we have the word of God was a human process, full of difficulties and open to perils. The process, of course, does not preclude the divine assistance but presupposes it. But such divine assistance did not obviate the need for the arduous and complicated human process. The choice of the New Testament canon, in other words, was not a miraculous process in the ordinary acceptation of the term.

A Summing Up

At this stage in the argument it is good to pause and see where we have been and where we are going. To what has been called a "fundamentalist" approach to the Bible, i.e., an approach that takes the Bible to be literally and inerrantly the word of God, a possible alternative is being proposed here. Such an alternative simply looks at how our Bible, more specifically our New Testament, came to be. It looks at the process of formation of our New Testament canon.

If God ever spoke to us through any prophet then he certainly spoke to us in Jesus Christ. But, unlike many prophets of old, Jesus did not leave behind a single written word. The words he spoke to the crowds in Palestine two thousand years ago were not, as far as we know, ever written down there and then by some recording secretary. Indeed, a reading of the New Testament leaves one with the distinct impression that Jesus of Nazareth was not particularly concerned to leave behind him an exact record of his discourses or instructions or revelations.

The words Jesus spoke to his contemporaries were remembered, but not in their entirety nor perfectly. They were, in the first place, not understood in identically the same way by everyone in the audience. Of course, those who believed in Jesus recalled his words and handed them down to other believers. But in that process they necessarily underwent selection, modification and adaptation to the changing needs of the time. In other words, if God spoke to us in Jesus Christ, then he chose ordinary human beings, with selective and fallible memories, with creative understanding and intelligence, to be the vehicles for that communication. Even when God spoke to us "in the Son" he allowed those words to be heard and remembered, preserved and utilized as human utterances and not as ready-made, immutable formulae.

It took time to gather and select the sayings of Jesus before incorporating them into our Gospels. It took time for the various writings of Saint Paul and the other authors of the New Testament to come to the attention of all the churches. But even then the recognition that this or that writing was to be regarded as "canonical" and considered a part of the Sacred Scriptures of the Christian churches was a process that was open to all the pitfalls and hesitations of human choice. As such it was not exempt from human error and shortcoming which, even if finally overcome, attended the process in its inception.

Thus, epistles were included as Paul's that Paul never wrote. Many sayings of Jesus never got into our four Gospels; and many others found there and attributed to Jesus would have been quite meaningless to his contemporaries in Palestine. Some writings that claimed to be from one or another of the apostles came to be included in the New Testament even though they were written years after the last apostle had died. The churches in Christendom were for centuries split over whether, for instance, the Epistle to the Hebrews and the Book of Revelation (the Apocalypse) were canonical or not. Some churches accepted Hebrews but rejected Revelation; others accepted Revelation but rejected Hebrews. Some churches persisted for a long time in regarding some clearly—at least to us today—non-canonical works as part of their Bible.

Such examples can be multiplied. But the ones cited should provide us with evidence of the great complexity of the whole process. Many areas in the history of the formation of our New Testament canon are, and are likely to remain, very obscure. The whole formation of our New Testament canon, i.e., of the twenty-seven books we consider as part of our Bible today, took centuries to complete and fix. The list underwent many changes and was, like all things human, subject to trial and error, to fallible human judgment, and to the changing needs of the times.

This fact alone, that we do have a New Testament which we believe to be the word of God to us despite all the evident limitations of the process of canonization, should be sufficient indication to most that God can and does communicate the mystery of his love for us through ordinary human means. Belief in the extraordinary and the spectacular is not necessarily the sign of great faith; and, even if founded on fact, not infallibly a sign of God's presence. The God of Jesus Christ can well be a God who lets the ordinary human process take its tortuous and unpredictable course.

Belief in this God must allow for his love to be no less real and operative in the early centuries than it is in later ones. Those who had a longer New Testament canon were not more loved by God than those who had a shorter one or, like most of the first generation of Christians, no New Testament canon at all. If that divine love can make room for error and misjudgment in the first centuries, then it can surely allow for them in our own time. A truly loving God can live with all this, with complex processes, imperfect historical data, uncertainties and defects and misunderstandings. It is man who will not.

It is we who refuse to accept this situation as we find it. It is we who imagine ourselves the beneficiaries of an inviolable, inerrant revelation of God, a revelation that overcomes the all too evident shortcomings of our fellowmen who were chosen to be the bearers of God's word to us. We seem to imply that we have a right to a fool-proof, letter-perfect, easily understood divine message. Nothing short of this, we protest, is worthy of our God; and nothing less than this, we imply, will do for us.

This, in the final analysis, is what a "fundamentalist" view of the Bible really involves. It chooses to forget, in practice if not always in theory, the complexity of the process that eventually, after many centuries, led to our New Testament. It is reluctant to consider all that was involved in the early Christians' affirmation that this or that work was the "word of God." In its insistence on the infallibility of that word it does not often pause to consider the implications of such a fact for the church of those illustrious centuries which, from our vantage point, did not always know where that word of God was, rejecting works that to us today are clearly and most emphatically Sacred Scripture, while accepting others that today are either relatively unknown to us or simply excluded from our canon.

The Text of the New Testament

Knowing what books properly belong in our Bible, however, is but the first step of many. For, even if God had dictated word for word the message of his revelation that has been preserved for us by the New Testament books, that written message has itself long since disappeared. We do not possess a single shred of papyrus, the writing material of the first centuries, containing a single line of a New Testament writing in the hand of its original author. All that we have are copies of the originals.

In this we are all debtors to thousands of copyists who, from one generation to the next, preserved and transmitted our sacred books to us. But they too of course were subject to human error. They misread some words, wrongly copied others, transposed whole sentences, skipped entire phrases, and made all the mistakes any one of us makes when we copy something. These were unwitting errors; and the ancient manuscripts of our New Testament are full of them.

But there were many other copyists who took it upon themselves to improve the imperfect grammar of some of the New Testament authors, to add explanations whenever something seemed to require clarification, or to introduce some changes in order to win some argument raging at the time. Many scribes relied here and there on their memory rather than on their sight, writing down what they remembered, not what they saw before them. Now these "corruptions" of our text of the New Testament are the legacy of Christian scribes who also believed that the Bible they were copying was the word of God.

Except for a few notes scattered here and there in our New Testament (e.g., "Other ancient authorities read. . . " or "Other ancient authorities omit . . . "), most of us are usually unaware of the incredible labors required to examine and compare the ancient manuscripts in order to "establish" the text of a given book, i.e., to get as close as humanly possible to what was written by Luke or John or Paul. Scholars, whose specialty is known as textual criticism, have to weigh and sift the accumulated evidence of thousands of manuscripts from the second to the fifteenth century. They have to evaluate evidence in favor of this word and against that, for including this phrase or omitting that, for judging this section as "authentic" and that as a later addition, etc.

The result of all these combined efforts gives us our New Testament text today. The work, to be sure, is done by recognized and respected experts in their field. But the result of their labor remains inevitably the product of human learning, fallible at times, often uncertain, frequently insufficiently informed. This, of course, does not give us a perfect text; but it does give us a text far superior to any literary remains from the distant past. Indeed, the text of the New Testament that we have today is far superior to very many more recent literary compositions.

Let us, for the sake of clarity, take a relatively simple example. The text of Matthew 5:21-22, already cited above, reads:

> *"But I say to you that every one who is angry with his brother shall be liable to judgment" (v. 22).*

The Revised Standard Version (RSV), the English translation of the Bible being used here and throughout this book, adds a footnote after the word "brother": "Other ancient authorities insert *without cause*." Now to read the verse as "angry with his brother without cause" is clearly quite different from reading it just as "angry with his brother." Those two words, "without cause," are very important. Yet all that the expert editors of the most recent edition of the New Testament in the original Greek can say about this is that there is "a considerable degree of doubt."

To those of us who are more frequently angry with our brother "without cause" than just merely angry, it certainly makes a good deal of difference which of the two statements is the word of the Lord. Moreover, this is one instance where we cannot very well say, as we are often inclined to do, that both one and the other are the words of Jesus in the Sermon on the Mount. We cannot dismiss this small point in the text as inessential either. It is quite essential for anyone of us human enough to have known anger and its bitter aftertaste.

Nevertheless, compared with other problems in the textual criticism of the New Testament, this particular one is quite minor. The matter is not quite so minor, however, when we are dealing with something as important as the account of the Last Supper in Luke 22:17-20. First of all, what is in question here is more than just a word or two. It involves the addition or the omission—depending on how you judge the evidence presented by the mass of manuscripts— of all the words within parentheses in the following quotation:

> *And he took bread, and when he had given thanks he broke it and gave it to them, saying "This is my body (which is given for you. Do this in remembrance of me." And likewise the cup after supper, saying, "This cup which is poured out for you is the new covenant in my blood") (Lk. 22:19-20).*

The words between the parentheses are a considerable and important part of the narrative. What Jesus did and said at the Last Supper is of no small significance for Christians. One would have expected that at least here some divine intervention would have come into play to guard the copyists against leaving Christian readers in such doubt at this particular point. After all, is a God who is eager to dictate his revelation literally and to guard his chosen messenger against all error unable to extend the necessary help to make sure that the message is copied without error, at least in its essential parts? If a prophet or an evangelist is divinely preserved against error, then it stands to reason that the scribe copying the "word of God" would be granted some help to transcribe it faithfully and without error. Alas! this is not the case.

Translation

But even if, by some truly extraordinary miracle, the words of Jesus were accurately handed on by word of mouth, scrupulously set down by an apostle, and faithfully copied by a succession of scribes and printers down to our own day, yet another peril attends its journey through the centuries.

Whatever the supposed or conjectured original language of one or another of our Gospels, all four of them in fact have come to us in Greek. Greek is the only record we possess of the words of the Lord in the New Testament. Evidently, therefore, we are dealing with a translation of the words of Jesus from their original Aramaic, which was the language Jesus and his contemporaries spoke in Palestine, into the current Greek of the first century.

There is, at this level at least, no real difficulty. Jesus could have made the revelation in Aramaic and the evangelists could have been inspired to set it down in Greek. The God who can reveal his mystery in Christ can equally well preserve its meaning intact in the four Gospels. Their authors, we maintain, were divinely inspired. The essential message in them is thus safeguarded and assured.

But most Christians today and for centuries past do not know and have not known any Greek at all. They always need a translation of the Greek of the New Testament into their own language. But—and here is one difficulty—translations are a mixed lot at best. You don't have to dismiss all translations with the Italian proverb, "Translators are traitors!", nor do you have to take as absolutely true the French's division of all translations into those that are faithful but ugly, and those that are beautiful but unfaithful to the original. You need simply be aware of the human limitations inherent in any translation, even the most competent.

To remove all the human limitations of a translation in such a way as to preserve the literal accuracy and beauty of the original message would require yet another miracle, another extraordinary intervention of the divine. This is not merely a postulate of common sense. Believing communities over the centuries have actually felt the need to invoke the presence of such divine help for their cherished translations of the sacred books.

Two rather different examples will illustrate this point. The language of the Jews who lived outside Palestine (the Diaspora) was Greek. Quite naturally they needed to have their Hebrew Torah translated into their language. Just as naturally they eventually came to claim a divine origin for the translation. They devised the legend of the seventy-two exemplary elders (hence the translation is called the Septuagint, from the Latin for "seventy") who did their work so accurately that, as the very ancient *Letter of Aristeas* tells us,

> *After the books had been read, the priests and the elders of the translators and the Jewish community and the leaders of the people stood up and said, that since so excellent and sacred and accurate a translation had been made, it was only right that it should remain as it was and no alteration should be made in it.*

It might be instructive to keep in mind that the New Testament authors quote the Greek translation of the Old Testament whenever they quote the Scriptures. Consequently, the debate on whether this Greek translation is inspired is by no means a dead issue even for Christians.

The second example concerns Christians more directly. The language of Rome was, of course, Latin; and so both the Old and the New Testaments were translated very early into that language. The Latin translations that circulated during the first few centuries were rather unsatisfactory; but continued use made them popular. It was not until the fifth century that the Western church got from the hands of Saint Jerome a Latin translation that eventually became "sacred." This is the version commonly referred to as the Latin Vulgate.

More than a thousand years after that translation was made, in 1546, the Council of Trent declared the Vulgate translation to be the one and only "authentic" translation for use in public reading, academic discussion, preaching and scriptural interpretation. The Roman Catholic Church's stand on this remained firm and unshakable. Until as recently as 1943 translations of the Bible into modern languages had to be made from the Latin Vulgate. Indeed, Catholics were not allowed to read any other translation even if it were made directly from the original Hebrew of the Old Testament and the Greek of the New. They had to wait for Vatican II before they could hear any really modern translation used in their liturgy.

Whatever qualifications one chooses to make in favor of the Catholic stand on the Vulgate, one has to take into consideration the fact that the Council of Trent pronounced a solemn anathema on anyone who dared to think that the Latin Vulgate "in all its parts" was anything but "sacred and canonical."

Thus, if one is to hold for a direct and literal inspiration of the word of God, one is in logic bound to extend the divine action to cover the translators as well as the prophets and evangelists. The Catholic Church is not the only Christian church to have reached that conclusion in its history. When other denominations state that the "word of God" says this or ordains that they rarely, if ever, have the Greek or the Hebrew original in mind. Moreover, one suspects, not all the opposition to any new English translation of the Bible today stems solely from sentimental attachment to the beauty and majestic cadence of the King James Version.

The Word of God to Me

There is still another complicating factor. Those who say of their Bible, "This is the word of God," usually imply that it is the word of God addressed directly to them. A very common, and quite understandable, conviction of many Christians is that the Bible is written with them in mind, that it speaks to them directly. From this they draw the conclusion that, because of this, the Bible can be read and understood by anyone who can read.

Often enough there is a closely allied conviction that the mere reading of the word of the Bible brings peace and comfort, strength and assurance to any believing reader. Many Christians speak often of "praying the Bible" or "meditating the Scriptures" or the "daily reading" of the Good Book. We do this with the conviction that this book has something to say to us here and now.

Such expressions reveal a very comprehensible and consistent attitude of the believer. If God speaks to man in an inerrant way, guaranteeing the literal accuracy of the message, then evidently God must have intended that word for all generations of believers and not for just a privileged few in the first century. So, the argument might proceed, this word of God is addressed to me in this twentieth-century metropolis every bit as much as it was addressed, say, to some Roman slave or a dock hand in Corinth.

However, it does not require very careful reading of, for example, the letters of Paul to realize that this is simply not so. Paul had the Philippians or the Corinthians or the Romans of the first century very much in mind. He addressed himself to their problems. He sought to reply to their questions. He appealed to their circumstances and was aware of their own particular situation. It would be naive, to say the least, for me to pretend that that situation, that set of circumstances, those questions and problems are mine today. Even if, by some stretch of the imagination, a similarity can be detected here and there, I must be careful to keep in mind how such similarity must be severely qualified and restricted.

If, to take a concrete example, Saint Paul's teaching on marriage and divorce is applicable to me here and now, I ought to make the necessary allowance for Paul's very different view of the family and family ties. I should keep in mind that the Corinthian Christians to whom Paul's instruction was addressed had a very different position in their society, held a different view of sex and marriage and, above all, had a very different attitude to the words of Paul than I do now. Paul certainly did not write the Epistle to the Corinthians as Sacred Scripture. The Corinthians did not read his words as the word of God to them, not when they first received the letter. That fact alone should give us pause before we affirm, without further qualification, that the word of the Bible is addressed to me here and now.

Interpretation

Every literary work is, of necessity, addressed to the author's contemporaries. It is addressed to a specific audience in a definite period of time and within a definite culture. We must not allow the poetry of our enthusiasm for some work of literature to deceive us into believing otherwise. In this sense, no author writes "for posterity"; no book is "timeless," not even the Bible. All masterpieces of literature, even of religious literature, are time-conditioned.

How many among the millions who read English as their native tongue today can read and fully understand a play of Shakespeare without some explanatory notes or a glossary of Shakespeare's vocabulary? Even fewer, I imagine, can read a slightly older author like Chaucer in anything but a "modern English" translation.

To pretend to read and understand a two thousand year old author of a Semitic background writing a sort of popular Greek in the first century is, for anyone in our situation, something of an impossibility. Even for someone who possesses the required linguistic skills and learning, the problem is only partially solved. In order to understand a document written two thousand years ago in a strange, and now quite dead, language one needs far more than the grasp of Greek grammar and the mastery of its syntax. What is needed is far more than even the very best translation in the world can possibly offer.

This brings us to still another difficulty that must be overcome on our way to understand what the word of God says to us in the Bible. The difficulty, perhaps the most serious of those discussed so far, is that of interpretation. Having as near a perfect translation as possible, I still need to understand what the words are actually saying. I need to grasp what those words, now rendered in readily accessible English, first said to the people who read them two thousand years ago before I can begin to glimpse what they might be saying to me.

With regard to this point, our situation is forever that of the finance minister of Candace, the queen of the Ethiopians, in Acts 8. On the desert road from Jerusalem to Gaza, Philip met him and, seeing that he was reading the prophet Isaiah, asked:

> *"Do you understand what you are reading?"*
> *"How can I, unless some one guides me?" (Acts 8:30-31).*

We always need a guide in reading not just the word of God but practically everything else we have to read. Even a daily newspaper report furnishes such guides when, for instance, it adds after a congressman's name his party and the state he represents. Usually, such information makes a great deal of difference in understanding what it is the congressman said.

A "guide" in our reading of the Bible is usually called an interpreter or an exegete. The task of such an interpreter (or exegete)
involves a twofold difficulty: First of all, everyone reads (or for that
matter hears) a spoken word against his own special background and
with his own set of presuppositions. Everyone of us brings to the
understanding of any text a whole set of judgments, prejudices,
questions and convictions. Thus, for example, the text quoted above
from Acts 8 cannot conceivably mean the same thing to a Christian
as to a non-Christian. It cannot be interpreted by a non-believer in
the supernatural as by someone who takes the supernatural as part
and parcel of life.

The problem with interpreting the incident in Acts 8 is far more
than that raised by its opening sentence:

But an angel of the Lord said to Philip . . . (Acts 8:26).

It involves far more than belief in angels. The incident, for its
proper interpretation, requires the reader's understanding of the
relation between the Old Testament and the New, between prophecy
and fulfillment. It also requires an idea of what "the good news of
Jesus" (Acts 8:35) is and how it can be understood.

The second difficulty involved in interpretation—and, in a way,
this is more peculiar to religious writing than it is to other literature—is that the interpretation of a text over the centuries is cumula-
tive. In this regard we are all, in the words Bernard of Chartres liked
to quote, "pygmies standing on the shoulders of giants." The "giants" for us in the Christian community are the Fathers and the
Doctors of the Church, the great saints and theologians, the reform-
ers and the founders of religious orders, the creeds and the councils,
the scholars and the preachers. This is what we call Christian
tradition. Everyone trying to understand what the Bible says to us
stands, consciously or unconsciously, somewhere within its vast and
variegated splendors.

So, when all is said and done, you need more than an understanding of your own background, the background against which a
biblical text was written, and the background of the interpreter who
interprets it for you. You need to know something of that tradition
within which both you and the interpreter who aids you read the

Bible. Ignorance of the background and the tradition must not be allowed to parade under the guise of impartiality.

"The Word of God in the Word of Man"

The purpose of this chapter so far has been to remind the reader of some of the implications of saying that our Bible is the word of God. It called attention to some of the very human factors that, of necessity intervene between the word of God and the one who hears or reads it. The factors, on the most basic level, involve the determination of what, in the midst of many rival claims, is the word of God and what is not, what is canonical Scripture and what is not. They involve also the process of copying, transmitting and establishing the sacred text; its translation into a modern language; and the interpretation needed to make even the translation comprehensible to someone thousands of years removed from the original composition.

Yet, someone might retort to all this line of argument, that the Catholic tradition at least had dealt comprehensively with these very human and fallible factors when it insisted that the Bible is the word of God in the word of man. The church thus safeguarded the absolute inerrancy of the essentials of the message and allowed a goodly margin of error for non-essentials.

But, however true such a statement about the Bible might in fact be, it really only advances the problem one step without solving it. It advances it by introducing a very useful distinction between the essential and the non-essential elements of the divine message. But this, far from solving the problem, adds yet another factor that inevitably affects the implications of our assertion that the Bible is the word of God. This added complicating factor is, of course, the question of what and who decides the essential and the non-essential in the divine message. Such a decision ultimately depends on what this or that community of believers, this or that church, this or that tradition regards as essential.

For, we must keep in mind, a Christian reading the Bible for whatever purpose always reads (or hears) it within a community. The community within which one reads or hears the word of God, the church which proclaims it, the tradition within which it is proclaimed, are all additional complicating factors. One need not be an expert historian or a professional theologian to realize how differently the various churches have understood such a basic assertion as "the Bible is the word of God." Even within one and the same church the understanding of the assertion has had a varied and checkered history.

For, even within a church that believes that the Bible is the word of God in the word of man and makes allowance for both, one has to understand how such an affirmation is to be interpreted. It can be regarded in a descending order: the word of God comes to a human author who gives it form and expression, and the believers accept it for what it is, the infallible word of God. Or it can be regarded in an ascending order: the community of believers accepts the writings of certain individuals as sacred to them and eventually comes to regard them as the word of God. It is, in other words, the faith of the community that gives these writings their privileged place. It is only after reflection that the community can say, and say without the shadow of a doubt, that these writings are "the word of God." But to anyone who does not believe in their God such writings are but part of the literary productions of ages past and no more.

In the final analysis, to affirm that a certain book is "the word of God" is to affirm what is not susceptible of proof the way a theorem in geometry can be demonstrated to be true. It is an affirmation that, ultimately, cannot be imposed from without. The freedom necessarily grounding our faith involves always the real possibility of its opposite. So, together with my gratitude for the faith I have that the Bible is the word of God must go my realization that, for very many in this world, the Bible is no more than "ancient literature."

Summary

We set out to propose an alternative to a descending view of what lies behind our statement that the Bible is "the word of God." We have concentrated our attention on the New Testament. Since we shall have occasion to deal with the words of Jesus as such in the next chapter, our description of the "ascending" process can begin with the canon, the list of books that (in both the Old and the New Testaments) are considered by Christians to be "Sacred Scripture," "the word of God."

The whole process of the formation of the canon, whether of the

Old Testament or the New, was not, in its initial stages, by an authoritative decree from above but by the choice of the believers themselves. It was believers who first accepted Jeremiah as a prophet. It was believers who first began to regard Paul's letters as an especially sacred document of the faith they professed in Jesus Christ. They used these documents in their worship of the Lord as Sacred Scripture long before any synod or council had declared them to be such.

Christian believers prized a certain writing enough to want it copied and diffused. They thought it worthy of reading in their liturgical assemblies. They had recourse to it as authoritative in their theological disputes and in attempting to explain the meaning of their faith to themselves and to others. Christians finally began to appeal to this work as they appealed to the "law and the prohets"; in other words, they considered it as "Sacred Scripture." The work was thus "canonized." When church authority, a few centuries later, published a canon of the Scriptures it was but acknowledging what the faith of the believers had already made a fact.

The implications of the inclusion, for instance, of the Epistle to the Romans in the canon of the Christian Bible became clearer in time. Christians argued that Paul, the author of the Epistle, must have been "inspired by God." What Paul wrote down is to us the true word of God. Because Paul was inspired by God to communicate to us his word, that word cannot contain error. So we speak of the Epistle to the Romans as the word of God.

Of course, this description is an oversimplification. The process varied with different books. The factors involved were far more complex than the above description would lead us to suspect. Our knowledge of the historical particulars in each case leaves something to be desired. But what is undeniable in all this is the direction of the whole trend to canonization: first the believers accepting and using a certain book, and then at the end of a long and tortuous road finally coming to regard it as the word of God.

We, from our point of vantage, can look back and ask: What was it that made the Christians choose the Epistle to the Romans and not, for example, that now lost first letter which Paul wrote to the Corinthians? The answer, however vague it might seem to some, has to be faith. It was faith that regarded a brief note jotted by Paul to

Philemon as the word of God. That that same faith chose the Second Epistle of Peter to be in the Christian canon and not, for example, those inspiring and lofty letters of Saint Ignatius of Antioch (written some years earlier than 2 Peter) can receive no completely satisfactory answer.

For, to pretend that the choice of the early Christians was divinely infallible and immune from error is to close one's eyes to the history of the formation of our canon. To claim for the early Christian believers exemption from hesitation, doubt and imperfect judgment is to claim for them what few if any of the authors of the New Testament enjoyed. Most of the New Testament authors were themselves ignorant of any such thing as a canonical Christian Scriptures. Our firmest confession of faith today must not blind us to the very human course of events that led up to the final formation of that canon. The God who became man would not be a mightier God for disdaining and bypassing ordinary human means however fallible and imperfect they might be.

This "ascending" view, however, carries within it a risk which cannot be evaded, to which the opposite view at first blush, seems to be immune. For the "descending" view knows, with the certainty of faith, that God can neither deceive nor be deceived. He reveals his message to a chosen messenger whom he inspires with the Holy Spirit and guards against all possible error, at least in essentials. In this view, the community of believers has only to accept those words for what they are: the true word of God. So any problems that arise—the risks involved, if you will—had better be left to the theologians. They have the business of explaining, if they wish, how the process took place and how its difficulties are to be solved.

The risk involved in holding an "ascending" view, on the other hand, is precisely the risk of accepting unequivocally that error factor which is involved in all things human. Christians espousing this view have to do without that pride which lures us into discoursing about the gradual dawning of the light of faith. Christians lived holy Christian lives and died, frequently enough, a martyr's death without our New Testament canon. Indeed, the first Christian generations really had no New Testament canon; those that followed them, a confused one; and many thereafter, an imperfect one. To this very day, Christian churches differ about the canon of the whole Bible.

In all this one has to remember that true Christian faith need neither deny human weakness nor transcend it. Human beings can, and usually do, believe the same way they think and the way they love: imperfectly. Attempts to bypass or leap over this fact are always futile. There has never been a "century of faith," an "age of reason," or a "season of love." All centuries, including the first, are centuries of belief and disbelief; all ages are ages of reason and irrationality; and, though love is never out of season, neither is its opposite.

Furthermore, a similar risk is run by all Christians, whatever understanding of the "word of God" they adopt, when the difficulties of the next step are considered. There is a risk of error always present and forever unavoidable in the preservation and transmission of the manuscripts of our Bible. That error is a permanent risk which human learning can minimize but never eradicate.

Some very significant texts, as for example the Lukan text on the institution of the Last Supper, will have to stand under a question mark. Some degree of doubt persists, and the debate continues. Even those most prepared to defend the longer text as an authentic part of Luke's Gospel will have to admit that theirs is a human judgment that will have to yield to better reason when such becomes available. Being on the side of the angels here does not exempt one from the possibility of error. It surely does not dispense one from the humility that becomes the Christian scholar.

The conviction that our Bible is the word of God involves taking into serious consideration the real hazards that beset the transmission of that word from one generation to the next. We can be sure, thanks to the incalculable scholarly labors of dedicated individuals, that the text of the New Testament we have today is far superior to anything that has come to us from the first century. Indeed, it is superior to much that has come down to us from more recent centuries. But this should not hide from us the fact that this New Testament text, what we call the word of God, is the result of human endeavor. It is made possible by the labor of scholars quite aware of the complexity and the limitations of the evidence with which they have to deal.

Another very human factor that must be kept in mind when we speak of the word of God is the factor of translation. There is no divinely inspired English translation, no matter how elegant or venerable. Whatever the claims that have been made and continue to be made for the Greek Septuagint or the Latin Vulgate, those of us limited to English have to realize that the best translation is the one which, while as faithful to the original as possible, makes it intelligible in today's English.

There is no perfect translation of the Bible. There is no English edition that is sacred. Every existing translation of the Bible, if it has not done so already, will become obsolete and will need replacement. Indeed, one of the most widely used English versions, the Revised Standard Version, is under constant revision. The latest edition of its New Testament, by the way, incorporates the words of Jesus in Luke 22:19-20, which the previous edition did not. This is by a decision of an editorial board, not by ecclesiastical decree; and it remains subject to change when a better argument or better evidence becomes available.

The reader of any translation of the Bible, moreover, must remember that every translation is, in its own way, an explanation of meaning, an interpretation. This, of course, is yet another very human factor that cannot be dismissed. Translators necessarily bring their own background and presuppositions to the text they translate. It might be convenient today to say that this or that English translation of the Bible was made under divine inspiration and guidance. But even such a translation, were it really to exist, would sooner or later need translation into more current and contemporary English than that of the age in which it was made. Such adaptation to the idiom of the day would, inevitably, require further interpretation by human authors.

We shall have an opportunity to consider this factor of interpretation later. For the moment it is enough to keep in mind what is implied in our saying that the Bible is the word of God by the fact that the formation of its canon has a history, its text needs to be established, and its original language requires translation into a modern idiom.

If you wish to adopt a "descending" view of the process then you must be ready to extend the series of divine interventions beyond the original inspiration of the prophet or the apostle. You must be willing to extend it to textual critics and copyists, to translators and interpreters.

If, however, you wish to adopt an "ascending" view of the process then it will be good to keep in mind, first, that it is not a new one at all. It is not a modern invention designed to undermine the faith of believers. Secondly, it is necessary to remember that this alternative view, no less than its opposite, believes in a God who can and does love human beings enough to reveal to them the mystery of his love. But, in this "ascending" view, God is seen as a God who loves human beings enough to leave them be what they are. God can tell the mystery of his love without having recourse to the extraordinary and the unusual. So, it seems a bit of a puzzle why Christians, who believe that God became man and was subject to all the limitations of human existence, should feel the need to exempt the word of God from such limitations.

Both views believe that God speaks to us and reveals himself to us. Both accept the Bible as divine revelation and as the word of God. They differ radically, however, in the way they understand this. The "descending" view insists on the divine inerrancy of the word; the "ascending' view insists on its human fallibility. This latter view refuses to eliminate the uncertainty and insecurity inherent in, and appropriate to, the acts of religious conviction. Such elimination would be ultimately impossible as the present chapter has tried to indicate.

In the final analysis, of course, the difference resides in the way each position understands the meaning of faith and the requirements for belief. But this difference is the subject of another book and the concern of a different question from the one with which this chapter deals.

2   The Word of Jesus

To a Christian nothing ever said by any prophet of old and nothing uttered ever since can even compare with the words of Jesus. Jesus is the definitive and final revelation of God to us. "In these last days," the Epistle to the Hebrews reminds us, God "has spoken to us by a Son" (Heb. 1:2). Naturally enough, whatever Jesus said, on howsoever insignificant a topic, has for us a value far exceeding all the learned distillations of wisdom past and present. Our desire and eagerness to discover any record of what Jesus said and taught is therefore more than understandable and certainly justifiable. And our New Testament furnishes us with just such a record.

Leaving aside all the difficulties alluded to or described in the foregoing chapter, we want to concentrate our attention in this one just on the words and teaching of Jesus as we have them in our Gospels. In order to do this, let us just suppose that the Greek text we have in our Gospels is beyond question, and its English translation beyond criticism. Even then, someone holding tenaciously to the view that we have in our Gospels the very words of Jesus will have to acknowledge the existence of a few problems. Such problems can best be described if we take some concrete examples.

(1) The Our Father is surely the Christian prayer par excellence. Matthew, in the course of the Sermon on the Mount (Mt. 6:9-13), gives us the words of the Our Father as we have learned to recite them when first we learned to pray. But Luke too gives us an Our Father that is slightly different (Lk. 11:2-4). His version, however, omits "Thy will be done, on earth as it is in heaven" and also "Deliver us from evil."

The differences between the two versions are not just of omission. Matthew prefaces the actual prayer by Jesus saying: "Pray then like this." Luke too, in a rather different setting, has the disciples asking

Jesus, "Lord, teach us to pray . . .," and Jesus responding to their demand with, "When you pray, say. . . ."

The easiest way to get around this particular discrepancy between the two accounts is to say that they tell of two different occasions when Jesus taught his disciples to pray, or that both accounts say much the same thing, or that the version given by Luke is just an abbreviated form of that found in Matthew.

But if we look a little more closely at the Gospels of Matthew and Luke (as we shall have occasion to do later) Luke's version of the Our Father is in all likelihood not an abbreviation at all. Rather it is Matthew's version that expands the original wording of the prayer. Such a tendency to make additions to the original prayer is also attested in a famous work from early Christianity, the *Didache,* as well as in several ancient manuscripts of our Gospels. It is in them that we find added to the words of the Our Father "for thine is the kingdom and the power and the glory, forever. Amen."

This expansion, by the way, is yet another illustration of what was said of textual criticism in the previous chapter. Today textual critics are agreed that the conclusion, "for thine is the kingdom . . .," is a later addition to the Gospel and not an original part of it. Yet, curiously enough, despite this practically unanimous judgment of scholars, Catholic and non-Catholic alike, the new Roman Catholic liturgical reform makes way for the spurious ending of the Our Father in celebrating the Eucharist.

A more serious difficulty arises, however, when we pretend that the two versions (that of Matthew and that of Luke) say much the same thing. We can set aside the considerable problem of translating accurately the petition for "our daily bread." For translators and scholars remain to this day quite uncertain whether the prayer says, "Give us this day *our daily bread*" or "our bread *for the morrow*" or perhaps something else still. Such difficulty is illustrative of the problem of translation and does not concern us at this point.

The difficulty that occupies us here is that of the real difference between the two versions. There is a clear difference between Matthew 6:12:

> *"And forgive us our debts,* as *we forgive our debtors"*

and Luke 11:4:

> *"and forgive us our sins* for *we ourselves forgive everyone who is indebted to us."*

It requires neither much learning nor great sophistication to realize that the difference between these two petitions is not minimal. It is not easy at all to reconcile both as two different versions of the same thing. In Matthew, the person praying is, ultimately, the norm and condition according to which God will accord forgiveness. In Luke, on the other hand, our forgiving others is the reason we give in asking for forgiveness.

The two prayers, even if given on two different occasions by Jesus, are not the same. The difference between Matthew and Luke is not just that of the setting in which Jesus teaches the prayer. Matthew and Luke give two very different understandings of the prayer itself.

In Matthew, Jesus follows the Our Father with:

> *"For if you forgive men their trespasses, your heavenly Father will forgive you; but if you do not forgive men their trespasses neither will your Father forgive your trespasses"* *(Mt. 6:14-15).*

The prayer is clearly a prayer of forgiveness; and that is how it is to be understood in Matthew. But in Luke the prayer is immediately followed by the Parable of the Friend at Midnight (Lk. 11:5-8), which illustrates the assured answer to prayer:

> *"And I tell you, Ask, and it will be given you; seek, and you will find; knock, and it wil be opened to you. For every one who asks receives, and he who seeks finds, and to him who knocks it will be opened"* *(Lk. 11:9-10).*

The Our Father in Luke is a prayer of petition, a prayer of confidence in the divine mercy.

You could say that the two different forms of the Our Father represent different attitudes to God. You could perhaps even say that Jesus provided two slightly different prayers for different occasions as they arose. But neither explanation obviates the problem of the actual practice of the churches. When was the last time you attended a religious service at which the worshiper beside you recited the Lukan version of the Our Father? The fact that we always use Matthew's version is but another example of the interpretation that always accompanies the word. The choice of one rather than the other form of prayer is, ultimately, a decision that in Matthew we have the words that "Our Lord taught us . . ."

(2) Few Christians are willing to dismiss the words spoken by Jesus at the Last Supper as unimportant. The event is a significant and momentous part of Jesus' life and the life of those who worship him as their Lord. What he said and did "the night before he suffered" is, evidently, of inestimable value to all Christians.

The fact that of all four Gospels only Matthew and Luke report the Our Father, the fundamental Christian prayer, need not greatly exercise us. But that the Gospel of John gives no account of the "Institution of the Lord's Supper" should at least give us pause. Yet, some might observe, our loss is made good by Saint Paul in 1 Corinthians 11:23-25. His account of the institution should compensate us for John's omission, even if it does not explain it.

But the omission by John is the least of our problems. We have already had occasion to refer to the problem we have in Luke's account of the Last Supper (Lk. 22:15-20): whether or not the last part of verse 19 and all of verse 20 belong to the original text of the Gospel or are a later addition. It will be best therefore to examine both possibilities:

A. If we say that verse 20 actually belongs after Luke 22:19 and reads:

> *And likewise the cup after supper, saying, "This cup which is poured out for you is the new covenant in my blood."*

then we have to face the problem of Jesus taking one cup in Luke 22:17-18 and saying:

> *"Take this, and divide it among yourselves; for I tell you that from now on I shall not drink of the fruit of the vine until the kingdom of God comes";*

then taking the bread and saying:

> *"This is my body" (v. 19);*

and then once again:

> *"likewise the cup after supper . . ."*

This, evidently, poses the problem of two cups used, one before and one after the supper. The words accompanying the first cup are much like those Jesus pronounces when he gives the cup to his disciples in Matthew 26:29 and Mark 14:25. So this raises a further question: whether one or both cups in Luke are "Eucharistic." This need not occupy us here; but the discrepancy in Luke's text must. This is no small matter. To be left in doubt as to whether or not one, two, or possibly three cups were passed around might be dismissed as academic. But can we so easily dismiss the problem of more than one *Eucharistic* cup in Luke's text?

Scholars can decide—and many have so decided—that the additional words in vv. 19 and 20 do in fact belong to Luke's original text. But such a decision is one reached after weighing the available evidence. It remains subject to change should newer or better evidence be found. So the following consideration of the alternative possibility is not altogether idle.

B. If we take the so-called "shorter" reading of the text in Luke and omit the last part of verse 19 and all of verse 20, then we are still left with the problem of the order of events. In Luke, Jesus first takes the cup and then the bread. In Paul, Mark and Matthew, Jesus takes the bread first. This order is, of course, the practice followed by the Christian churches.

Surely here we cannot say there were two *Last* Suppers. So the question we have to ask is: Did Luke make a mistake or were Paul and the two evangelists misled? Even if we try to reconcile, as many have tried to do, all the accounts and harmonize them, using all that we know about the Jewish Passover practices and every bit of learning that can aid us, it would still remain a grave problem. The procedure of the Lord's Supper will ultimately have to rest on either human option or human opinion. What Jesus did or did not do at the Last Supper might be settled by an authoritative decree or by ecclesiastical practice. But, short of claiming divine inspiration for one or the other, our problem remains really unsolved.

The problem is: How do you read the Lukan account of the institution of the Lord's Supper "literally and inerrantly"? What, in the final analysis, were the very words of Jesus at the Last Supper? Which, if any, were not his own words but later additions by zealous and well-meaning Christians? If there were some additions made, then how do we explain their attribution to Jesus by a "divinely inspired" author?

The series of questions can be extended and, I imagine, some answers to them can be devised. But the point that is being made here is that, even in important matters like Christian prayer and the Lord's Supper, the very words of Jesus remain beyond our grasp. The ultimate decision, if there be any, as to what Jesus said in either case will have to depend on human ingenuity and the competence of experts and scholars in the New Testament. They, alas, are not exempt from error and rarely claim to be divinely inspired.

(3) The third and final example is briefer and less complicated than the first two. Both Matthew and Luke give a series of Beatitudes pronounced by Jesus at the beginning of the Sermon on the Mount (as it is in Matthew) or the Sermon on the Plain (as it is in Luke). The first Beatitude in Matthew reads:

> *"Blessed are the poor in spirit; for theirs is the kingdom of heaven" (Mt. 5:3);*

and that in Luke:

> *"Blessed are you poor, for yours is the kingdom of God" (Lk. 6:20).*

Now the difference between the two is not just that of the generic third person in Matthew and the very specific "you" addressed to the disciples in Luke. The real difference is in what is being said and not just to whom.

There is, evidently, a great difference between being "poor in spirit" and being simply "poor." Even if one were to imagine a similar sermon delivered by Jesus in two different places and to two different audiences, one still cannot evade the difficulty created by "poor" and "poor in spirit."

Who precisely is the object of the blessing pronounced by Jesus? The poor, dispossessed, destitute followers of Jesus? or all those who, in the midst of plenty, are not slaves to their possessions, are so indifferent to their wealth that they live a life of detachment which can best be described as "poor in spirit"?

Here again, as in the other example cited above in chapter 1 (the "angry with his brother" or "angry without cause" in Mt. 5:21), if

Jesus is teaching some religious truth, then it does make a great deal of difference what he actually said. If we are going to pattern our lives on the first Beatitude then we had better make sure which of the two we choose. Both of them cannot be taken together and harmonized. They actually cancel one another out.

The whole idea behind the search for Jesus' words is that we think it impossible for him to deceive us. Anyone capable of saying Matthew's Beatitude to one group and Luke's to another cannot very easily escape the charge, if not of outright deception, then at least of temporizing. This is hardly acceptable to any Christian, least of all to those who insist that in the Gospels we have the very words of Jesus speaking to us.

The more sophisticated reader of the New Testament might devise a way out of the difficulty by saying that the two statements are illustrations by Jesus of that justice toward all that the Holiness Code teaches in the Book of Leviticus:

> *"You shall not be partial to the poor or defer to the great"*
> *(Lev. 19:15).*

This could, conceivably, provide an escape from the difficulty were it not for the fact that, in Luke's Gospel, Jesus makes his position unequivocally clear by adding to the "Blessed are you poor" (Lk. 6:20):

> *"Woe to you that are rich, for you have received your consolation" (Lk. 6:24),*

which, on any reading, shows clear partiality to the poor.

Summing Up

The three examples cited above can be multiplied, of course. Solutions too can be found to the problems they pose. But the point to be kept in mind in our discussion is this: If the Gospels are a faithful record of the very words of Jesus, then those words are a source of innumerable problems, contain a good deal of ambiguity, and require more than a perfectly preserved text and an impeccably translated New Testament to have them speak to us directly. They require interpretation; and that interpretation, unless miraculously preserved from error, is an inevitably fallible and humanly conditioned factor interposed between the "word of the Lord" and the believer.

An ecclesiastical institution could, of course, settle the dispute authoritatively by saying this or that is the only true interpretation. But even the Roman Catholic Church, which has never lacked boldness in stating and defining its divine prerogatives, has been extremely slow and reluctant to define the meaning of such specific biblical texts.

Individuals, with or without the learning and expertise needed, often insist that this is what Jesus actually said or taught. But, in view of the problems involved in such an assertion, it is not very clear what its basis is. To choose Matthew's version over Luke's, or Luke's over Mark's as the one having the exact words of the Lord is an act of interpretation. It is, moreover, the choice of my own interpretation, howsoever profound the faith that inspires it, against the words of an author I confess to be divinely and inerrantly inspired precisely to communicate to me God's word.

Alternative Approach

Here too, as we did in the first chapter, we can take a different approach that would enable us to understand what it is we actually have when we say we have the word of the Lord in our Gospels. The best way to do this is, once again, to see how our Gospels came to be. In order to do this, we shall try to describe, without going into all the technicalities and details, a method that is commonly called Form Criticism.

Our New Testament is a collection of a variety of literary documents. The Gospels, though unique in many ways, are themselves literary documents and can therefore profit much from what we have learned about all literary composition. The investigation of the Gospels has learned a great deal from work done by scholars in the nineteenth century on the Old Testament. Those Old Testament scholars had in turn learned a great deal from the work done on the literary remains of antiquity.

This method of reading and understanding the Bible, after a long resistance on the part of ecclesiastical authorities, received official sanction from Pope Pius XII in his 1943 encyclical on Sacred Scripture. It received even more solemn approval in the Dogmatic

Constitution of Vatican II on Divine Revelation. Catholics would do well to read carefully the third chapter of that Constitution on "The Divine Inspiration and the Interpretation of Sacred Scripture."

The Teaching of Jesus

When Jesus spoke and preached to the people of Palestine in the first century, his audiences naturally remembered his words as people do the words of a great teacher. But, just as naturally, they forgot some of what Jesus said, misinterpreted or misunderstood others. No two human beings listen to and understand the same speaker in identically the same way. How much more true this would be if the speaker were God. Of course, no Jew in Palestine of the first century—or of any other century for that matter—would for a moment believe that a man, speaking ever so eloquently and authoritatively, is God himself speaking to him. That might conceivably happen in the pagan world (see, for example, Acts 14:11-13, where Paul and Barnabas are called "gods"); but never in monotheistic Judaism.

It was only natural then that those who listened to Jesus heard him with just ordinary human attention, retained his words as one might the words of a great teacher, and recalled them with a power of recall subject to all the vagaries of human memory. Even if they had fully realized who it was who spoke to them, could they have done otherwise?

After the Resurrection of Jesus, when those who believed in him began to comprehend who he was and what he meant to the world, it was only natural that their new-found faith generated the zeal to go and proclaim him to everyone. They set out to win others to "the Way" (Acts 9:2). In doing this, they were, naturally enough, eager to tell everyone what Jesus taught and what he did in order to win converts to the new faith.

The first believers were just what we call "ordinary folk," neither sophisticated scholars nor learned members of academies. Their remembrance of what Jesus taught and their handing it on to others was subject to what is often called "folk memory." The workings of such memory are not entirely unknown to us. Ordinary people, by and large, do remember things in certain fixed ways and, often unconsciously, employ almost standard memory gimmicks to recall them.

Folk memory preserves best the small detached units: a brief saying, a proverb, a short story with a punch line, etc. It also tends to keep such items in patterns that facilitate their recall: a pair of sayings having a common idea or a common word, two contrasting sayings, etc.

Moreover, when people recall a story or quote a saying, they do so, normally, for some purpose or with a reason. Yet, in the most perfunctory quotations, there is continual adaptation and modification. The reasons why something is retold keep changing, the purpose for which it is retold does not remain fixed. A word is changed here, something is added there, a situation is slightly altered to suit a different audience, etc. Anyone who has ever told a story more than once should require no convincing that this is indeed so.

We realize, of course, that all this is necessary simply because a dialogue between two human beings is instinct with life and marked by the individuality of both the speaker and the hearer. Even when the words of such a dialogue are set down and fixed in writing in some literary composition, every attentive reader will have noticed that life is forever breaking through and disrupting the illusory neatness of the communication.

The words of Jesus, in the early stages of their preservation and oral transmission by those who believed in him, were every bit as subject to the peculiarities of ordinary human memories as is anything else. Respect for, even adoration of, Jesus did not and could not subtract his words from the human process of recall and retelling. His followers had many reasons for citing his words. But so far as we can judge at this distance in time, none of the reasons was the simple preservation of every syllable of each word uttered by the Master. The followers of Jesus were not transmitting consecrated formulae but keeping a dialogue with their contemporaries open and alive.

The words of the Master, to be sure, were quoted; but they were quoted for different purposes. The Christian community sought to win new converts to their faith. They had to instruct the converted and respond to their questions. They had to enlighten the honest inquirers and be ready to answer their questions. Opponents of the new religion as well as supporters listened to them. Native Palestinian Jews were the greater part of Jesus' audiences. His followers had to address citizens of different lands and dwellers of no mean cities. To repeat what Jesus said, faithfully and word for word, without adaptation and without explanation, would not only have been ineffectual but completely unintelligible.

Moreover, the Jesus who addressed the crowds and instructed his disciples was to most of them just "the carpenter's son" (Mt. 13:55; Mk. 6:3). But the Jesus whom the primitive band of believers proclaimed was the Risen Lord. To say that his own disciples could have heard the very same words in the same way before and after the Resurrection is not to extol the power of God but to misunderstand the central mystery of the Christian faith. After the Resurrection of Jesus the most ordinary word and the most insignificant of his gestures assumed a radically different meaning for the believers. It was that meaning that they went out to proclaim to the world.

The Gospels

Let us now leap ahead in time to our Gospels in order to see what happened to those words that Jesus spoke. We must recall at the outset that our Gospels are, to a great extent, made up of small individual units called "pericopes." Thus a parable, or a healing performed by Jesus, or a miracle recounted by a Gospel usually constitutes a pericope. The various sections read from the Scriptures on a Sunday are usually pericopes. Most of the pericopes in our Gospels are self-contained units that can be removed from their present setting and examined individually.

Following the example of Old Testament scholars before them, New Testament scholars early in this century began to investigate the literary form of these individual pericopes. A parable is a different literary form from a proverb; a miracle of nature like the stilling of the storm at sea is a different literary form from a healing story; the cure of a blind man is a different literary form from an exorcism.

These pericopes, prior to their inclusion in our Gospels, enjoyed a life of their own in the oral tradition of the early Christian community. They were, more often than not, passed on by word of mouth. Their different literary forms, moreover, reflect different situations in the life of the community that preserved them. The situation that called forth the telling of the Parable of the Sower by Jesus was not the same as that which caused his followers to remember and retell it. That later situation is different still from the one that prompted Mark to include the Parable in his Gospel.

Perhaps an everyday example will help illustrate this better. A joke is a literary form with which we are quite familiar. Most people know that a funeral service is not usually the place to tell a joke. You don't have to be an ancient sage to know that there is "a time to weep, and a time to laugh" (Eccles. 3:4). On the occasion when a joke is told we can readily classify it as a war joke, a sick joke, a drunk joke, or a shaggy dog story. We can, moreover, usually guess the original purpose (political, racial, sexual, etc.) behind a particular joke almost as quickly as we can figure out why it is being told at this particular point to this audience. This is why, often enough, after I laugh at a joke I add, "OK! I get it."

The joke in our everyday usage can give us some idea of what happens to oral traditions in the course of their transmission. A parable, which is another form of popular literature, told by Jesus is understood by his hearers against the background of its telling and in the particular situation in which it is told. That background and that situation are usually forgotten in the retelling of a parable. The retelling, moreover, has a different reason and, in all likelihood, a very different purpose. It is also quite possible that no two hearers of the original parable recall it the same way or for the same reason. All these factors conspire to put the original meaning of the parable at several removes from us, the present hearers.

The Parable of the Sower

Let us take the well-known Parable of the Sower. We have it in three Gospels: Matthew 13:1-9; Mark 4:1-9 and Luke 8:4-8. It is particularly useful as a New Testament example because there is an interpretation to go with it in Matthew 13:18-23; Mark 4:13-20 and Luke 8:11-15. It would take us too far afield to go into all the details. Let us just compare the ending of the parable in the three versions. The seed that falls on good soil achieves the following results: in Matthew: "some a hundredfold, some sixty, some thirty"; in Mark: "thirtyfold and sixtyfold and a hundredfold"; in Luke: "a hundredfold."

Obviously, if only because of this important concluding line, the parable varies greatly from one Gospel to the other. Matthew's seems to indicate the great diversity of the results; Mark's, the steady increase and growing success; and Luke's, the assured yield. We could speculate about the purpose for which the parable was told and retold in the oral tradition prior to its incorporation into our Gospels. By comparing all three versions, we can even try to reconstruct the situation that required the recall and the retelling of the parable. Finally, in theory at least, we can push it back all the way to the situation that made Jesus tell it and so reconstitute, as it were, "the very words of the Lord."

But, even if we were to succeed in this undertaking, what shall we do with the three very different interpretations that go with the parable? Every interpretation is prefaced by Jesus himself saying, "Hear then the parable of the sower ..." (Mt. 13:18); or "Do you not understand this parable? How then will you understand all the parables?" (Mk. 4:13); or "Now the parable is this ..." (Lk. 8:11). As in the parable itself, the interpretation which each evangelist provides reflects a peculiar situation and answers a special need of the community that listened to it. The listeners, new disciples of Jesus, attended to these words as the words of the Lord Jesus to them there and then. They were not a society of antiquarians verifying records; they were a community of believers responding to a call.

The Jesus who told the Parable of the Sower for the first time had a definite purpose and addressed a specific situation. He was not dictating memoirs for posterity. Those who went about proclaiming his message repeated the parable; but they had a different purpose in telling it and faced a new situation. If nothing else, the original teller of the parable had died and risen from the dead; and that in itself altered the situation radically.

The Christian preachers of the first century were aware that they were not repeating by rote what the Master *had said* on this or that occasion. They were conscious that they were addressing their fellow Christians and prospective converts with what Jesus *is saying* to them here and now. The "words of the Lord" were not a report; they were an address.

Now, as the words of Jesus were used over and over again, their repeated usefulness naturally varied with the different needs that arose within the community and without. Some words of Jesus were used in the liturgical assemblies of believers; others in debates and disputes with non-believers; others in catechetical instructions of future converts, etc. Each different situation colored the use of the particular pericope, modified its form and adapted its application. Nothing in what Jesus said could escape this process. The Christian message did not depend on the repetition of consecrated formulae but on living a life that was a faithful response to a challenge.

When the preachers went out to proclaim the message their purpose was not to achieve an exact word-for-word reproduction what the Master had said. It was to confront their hearers with a fact. On the day of Pentecost, when Peter finished his inaugural proclamation of the Christian message (Acts 2:14-36), the people asked:

"Brethren, what shall we do?"

Peter's response was not "Now repeat after me . . ." It was rather:

"Repent, and be baptized every one of you in the name of Jesus Christ for the forgiveness of your sins" (Acts 2:38).

Form Criticism

Early in this century New Testament scholars came to see that the different forms of the tradition about Jesus, like all oral tradition everywhere, had a history. The use of a given parable, for instance, can reflect the various situations that its telling passed through before it came to be incorporated into our Gospels. We can surmise the purpose to which this saying of Jesus or that parable was put by the primitive community of believers. We are, in other words, willing to see the word of Jesus as a living word, addressed to real human beings in concrete life situations.

Such a procedure in the study of our Gospels is then an investigation of the history of the literary forms that are in them. It is commonly called Form Criticism.

Form Criticism recognizes that before you interpret any saying of Jesus, before you can say what it means, you have to know what its "literary form" is, whether the saying is a proverb or a parable, a polemical saying or a moral exhortation. This step in the procedure simply recognizes a common everyday practice. We all know, at least implicitly, that it does make a great deal of difference, for example, if we read a comic strip as a little comedy, a political comment, or a social satire.

Form Criticism, moreover, accepts the fact that our Gospels are made up of individual units which, prior to their incorporation into the Gospels, had an independent life of their own as oral traditions about Jesus, his words and his deeds. As such, these pericopes were subject to the factors affecting the oral transmission of popular literature.

Finally, Form Criticism also underlines the fact that the various forms reflect very concrete and real situations in the life of the early Christian community. It was those situations that required the recall and retelling of this or that saying and ultimately preserved it for posterity.

The Synoptics

Now, it is these individual traditions about Jesus that are incorporated in our Gospels, which are for us the richest source for the words and the teaching of Jesus. Evidently then, these Gospels must claim our attention at this point in our attempt to understand what we mean when we say, "This is the word of the Lord!"

It is necessary to concentrate our attention, however, on the first three Gospels. The Gospel of John is, in many ways, a case apart; and we shall have occasion to devote attention to it later.

There is something peculiar about the first three Gospels. They can be arranged, relatively easily, into three parallel columns that allow us to see how they tell the same story, recount the same miracle, or retell the same parable, but all in slightly different ways. Such an arrangement is called a "synopsis." And, naturally enough, the first three Gospels are called the *Synoptic* Gospels.

A study of a Gospel Synopsis (from the Greek for "to view together") will reveal, even to the untrained eye, extensive similarities between Matthew, Mark and Luke. Upon closer inspection, the similarities will be seen to extend beyond the order of events to actual similarity in details and even to close identity in language. It has been pointed out, for example, that of the 677 verses in Mark's Gospel only sixty or seventy are not found in Matthew and Luke. In Matthew and Luke, which are both much longer than Mark, there are some 200-220 verses that have no parallel in Mark. Most of these verses, moreover, are sayings of Jesus.

This is a strange phenomenon indeed. We have three works, written by three different people living in different places and writing at different times, all of them showing close similarity, often verbal identity, with each other. The most obvious, almost inevitable, explanation is that somehow they are dependent on each other. But it is not that easy to ascertain the order of their interdependence. Did Matthew come first and then Mark and then Luke, as we find them in our New Testament? Or is there another, more satisfactory order of dependence?

As might readily be imagined, very many hypotheses have been proposed. Of these, the most commonly accepted and widely used hypothesis today is that called the two-source hypothesis. Its wide acceptance and common use by New Testament scholars are in large measure due to the fact that it explains most of the difficulties satisfactorily and leaves the least number of unsolved problems. It remains, however, a hypothesis, albeit a highly workable one.

In this hypothesis, Mark's Gospel is seen as one of the two principal sources used by both Matthew and Luke. They both follow Mark's order of events. They might differ among themselves on a given point. One of them might differ with Mark on some detail. But Matthew and Luke seldom join in differing on a point with Mark Such facts are best explained if we say that Matthew and Luke used Mark as a source; and they would be hardest to explain if, for instance, we were to insist that Matthew came first and then Mark and Luke followed him.

The second source in the two-source hypothesis is postulated in an attempt to explain those 200-220 verses that are absent from Mark but are common to Matthew and Luke. The verses include the Our Father, the Beatitudes, and very many sayings of Jesus. The postulated source for them is called, by common convention, "Q." This is, of course, a hypothetical source since we do not possess a written document that we can actually point to as "Q."

That such a document as "Q" was a written source used by Matthew and Luke is made necessary by the fact that so many of the verses common to both are word-for-word the same. When differences occur between them they can be satisfactorily and consistently explained within each Gospel. You can, for example, find a reason for the differences we pointed to above in the first Beatitude in Matthew and Luke; and that difference can be shown to be consistent with what Luke usually does with the sayings of Jesus.

Our two-source hypothesis then implies the priority in time of Mark over both Matthew and Luke. But postulating this priority of Mark goes counter to a very old and venerable tradition that maintained Matthew's to have been the first Gospel written. He was followed by Mark, who gave us an abbreviated version of the first Gospel. In other words, tradition insists that the order in which we find the Gospels in the New Testament today is the order in which they were composed.

This tradition, of course, cannot be dismissed lightly. If the literary tools and the historical information available to us make the tradition untenable, then it would need more than age or repetition to make it prevail. Today, as a matter of fact, the vast majority of New Testament scholars, Catholic and Protestant alike, take the priority of Mark for granted as a working hypothesis in their study of the Synoptic Gospels.

Thus, the two-source hypothesis and the priority of Mark, which were part of the legacy of nineteenth-century scholarship to the study of the Gospels, have become today the common basis for the study of the Synoptics. For, when the history of the literary forms in these Gospels finally came under consideration, the interdependence of the Synoptics and the priority of Mark became more and more necessary as working hypotheses for their interpretation.

Scholars came to realize that the traditions about Jesus were, so to speak, frozen in a stage of their development when they were collected in "Q" or included in the Gospel of Mark. But, as someone has pointed out, the oral tradition about Jesus did not suddenly stop the day Mark wrote his Gospel. Those traditions, like all living traditions, continued to grow and develop. Some traces of them have come down to us in the writings of the early Christian Fathers and also in a large mass of "apocryphal" Christian literature like the recently discovered Gospel of Thomas. Most of these traditions are sayings of Jesus.

What is important to see in all this is how a certain saying of Jesus can be reported by all three evangelists, modified by each, and made to serve a specific purpose dictated by the situation which each addressed. By comparing one Gospel with another (and, when possible, by comparing them with sources outside the New Testament like the Fathers or the apocryphal literature), New Testament scholars can often enough make a very good guess at what the particular saying of Jesus might have been in its oral stage, prior to its incorporation into one of our Gospels. But, of course, this line of argument still leaves us with the need to go beyond the oral tradition to the first and most important stage of all: that of what Jesus himself said and the situation he addressed.

The difficulty of such a procedure can best be illustrated by an actual saying of Jesus reported by all three evangelists and in very similar contexts. After Peter's confession at Caesarea Philippi, Jesus predicts his passion and instructs his disciples on what being a follower of him really means (Mk. 8:27-38; Mt. 16:13-27; Lk. 9:18-26). Then, according to Mark, Jesus adds:

> *"Truly, I say to you, there are some standing here who will not taste death before they see* the kingdom of God come with power" *(Mk. 9:1).*

This last phrase in Matthew 16:28 reads:
> *"the Son of man coming in his kingdom";*

and in Luke 9:27:
> *"the kingdom of God."*

This, surely, is a momentous statement. Its meaning can deeply affect our understanding of what Christ's work was and what Christianity should be. Yet, even if after very close examination of the Gospel texts scholars conclude that Matthew and Luke were the ones who modified the form of the saying found in Mark, the crucial question is still: Where did Mark himself get these words of Jesus? If from the oral tradition, then did he modify them as Matthew and Luke after him did? Supposing you can argue successfully that Mark got the words from the oral tradition and reported them unaltered, then you still have to find out what purpose the saying served in that early Christian community which preserved the saying orally. Was the expression used with reference to the Resurrection of Jesus? to his coming to this earth? to his return at the end of time? or to something else altogether? But, even after we tackle these questions successfully, we are left wondering what it was Jesus said originally and, if he said it, what he meant by it.

It hardly needs stating here that the saying is in itself no trifling matter. Christians would certainly be interested in knowing what Jesus said on this occasion and more important still, exactly what he meant by seeing "the kingdom of God come with power." For all the "democratic" tendencies of our modern jargon, the "kingdom" still seems to enjoy some force in Christian dialogue. At least we still pray daily, "Thy kingdom come." What then are we praying for? What is it Jesus himself wanted us to ask for? Has this kingdom come? is it going to? or is it now coming?

The Quest for the Words of Jesus

The attempt to go back to the very words of Jesus, back from Mark to the oral tradition of the primitive Christian community, and from that tradition back to Jesus himself, is quite comprehensible and certainly justifiable. Some scholars have gone so far as to formulate norms by which we can judge, out of that creative welter of early Christian traditions, the authentic words of Jesus. Indeed, some have even thought that, based on these authentic words, they could reconstruct what Jesus himself thought of himself and how he understood his mission. So these norms call for some brief examination at least.

The norms purpose that (1) if a certain saying is quite unlike anything that we know in the Judaism of the time of Jesus and not very suitable for the early church's purpose; (2) if that saying fits into the overall picture of the teaching of Jesus; and (3) if the saying is attested to by more than one source, then that saying has every chance of being an authentic saying of Jesus.

Let us illustrate this procedure by two different examples:

A. Origen, the Christian Father of the third century, reports a saying of Jesus not recorded in any of our Gospels but found in the apocryphal (non-canonical) Gospel of Thomas, which is just a collection of sayings of Jesus (very much, perhaps, like the source "Q" mentioned above). The saying runs:

> "He that is near me is near the fire; he that is far from me is far from the kingdom."

Let us suppose for the sake of the argument that this saying meets the first and the third conditions: the first, because it seems quite unlike anything a Jewish rabbi of the first century would say; and the third, because, though not literally there in any of our canonical Gospels, it does find close echoes in Mark 9:49:

"For every one will be salted with fire,"
and Mark 12:34:
    "You are not far from the kingdom of God."
But is the saying "characteristic" of the teaching of Jesus? Does it fit into the whole picture?

One modern author states unhesitatingly, "There can be no doubt that this has the ring of a genuine saying of Jesus." The question is: How does one acquire an ear for "the ring of a genuine saying of Jesus"? Can one really sift the many words of Jesus in our Gospels and arrive at the "genuine" items without some prior understanding of who Jesus really was? without some notion of what Jesus had to be like? In other words, a certain understanding of Jesus is really the determining factor which none of the three formulated norms acknowledges. Such understanding, by howsoever scholarly or saintly a mind, is ultimately yet another human interpretation, very limited and quite subject to amendment, not to say error. All of us, however well-meaning, are inclined to create a Jesus, if not in our likeness then certainly to our liking.

There is an added concern for us here. If Jesus did actually say these words, are they therefore the "word of God" for us even though they are not recorded as such anywhere in our canonical New Testament? Would they carry the same authority as the enigmatic words in Mark 9:49 about being "salted with fire"? Such questions might not occupy the thoughts of all the scholars trying to discover the words of Jesus; but they have to occupy those who quote "the word of the Lord."

B. The second example is from the New Testament itself. In Acts 20:35 Paul, addressing the elders of the church of Ephesus, says:

> *"In all things I have shown you that by so toiling one must help the weak, remembering the words of the Lord Jesus, how he said, 'It is more blessed to give than to receive.'"*

Let us here assume once more that this saying meets the first and the second norms, being sufficiently extraordinary and fitting into Jesus' exhortation to love one another. But we do not have this saying recorded elsewhere in our New Testament. Is it therefore to be rejected for lack of "multiple attestation"? or is it to be accepted simply because we believe the Book of Acts to be the word of God and so cannot state what is not true?

The above two examples were cited to illustrate the great difficulty we encounter in trying to apply the norms proposed by some or any other norms we might wish to devise. The reason the first norm was so readily granted in both examples is precisely the extreme difficulty of its application. The world of first-century Judaism is complex and constantly surprising us with new discoveries. The "primitive Christian community" too is no easy thing to reconstruct. It is at best a handy cipher for referring to a small seed in a vast germination of religious ideas. So it is not so easy to judge whether or not a saying of Jesus is part of, or completely different from the prevalent traditions of the first century.

The third norm is perhaps the easiest to apply since it deals with written evidence. But, here too, what are we willing to admit as evidence? The four Gospels only? all the writings of the New Testament? the early Christian Fathers? all the available writings of the first three or four centuries? Even if a decision on such matters can be reached, who is it who reaches it? The scholars because of their learning? the church by reason of its God-given authority? or we the believers whose "hearts burn within us" (Lk. 24:32) whenever we hear a genuine word of Jesus?

The second norm, the norm of "consistency," as it has been called, is the most difficult to apply, as we have already seen. It does require a prior understanding of what Jesus could or could not have said. You have to have some idea of what is "characteristic" of the teaching of Jesus before you decide what fits into it and what does not. To say that a saying of Jesus has a "genuine ring" to it is to pretend that the whole process described above has been satisfactorily carried to its conclusion. It is to suppose that we actually can move beyond our Gospels to the early Christian community and beyond it to Jesus of Nazareth and his revelation of God's love for mankind.

But we cannot. Our inability comes not from any defect in the faith we profess in Jesus Christ as the revelation of God but from the way we choose to understand that faith. There can be, in other words, another way to understand what we have in our Gospels when we read, "And the Lord said . . . ."

3   The Living Word

One of the most disconcerting facts encountered in our study of the New Testament is the prevalent anonymity of its authors. With the sole exception of Saint Paul, we do not know with certainty who the authors of our New Testament books were. The titles usually assign an author to each book; and we speak of Mark writing this or Matthew saying that, but these are really conventions of convenience.

Thus, for example, the title of the first book in the New Testament is "The Gospel according to Matthew." But this does not really tell us who this Matthew was. That Matthew 9:9 recounts the vocation of Matthew and that Matthew 10:3 lists "Matthew the tax collector" among the twelve apostles do not argue that this is the same person to whom the title ascribes the first Gospel. So similarly with the other Gospels and books of the New Testament.

Tradition has held that the books of the New Testament were written by the authors whose names they bear. But we have to ask whether this tradition is immune from error. There are ample, and very compelling, reasons for thinking that, except for some letters of Paul, the authors of our New Testament books are unknown to us.

Until very recently, tradition held that the Epistle to the Hebrews was written by Saint Paul. Nowadays, not even Roman Catholics are bound to hold that Paul is the author of Hebrews the same way he is the author, say, of Romans. It would be very difficult indeed for most New Testament scholars today to describe Paul as in any way an "author" of Hebrews.

The title of another New Testament book is "The Second Epistle of Peter," and its opening words read, "Simon Peter, a servant and apostle of Jesus Christ" (2 Pet. 1:1). Yet, judged by all the literary and historical evidence we can muster, 2 Peter gives every evidence of having been written at least half a century after Saint Peter's martyrdom.

Similarly, Revelation 1:4 says: "John to the seven churches that are in Asia"; but that does not mean, as tradition has maintained, that this is necessarily the John who wrote the Epistles of John, who wrote the Gospel of John, and who was "the beloved disciple." One could at least object that there must have been more than one John in the first century.

The problem, illustrated in the above examples, extends beyond the inclusion of the title of a given New Testament book under the aegis of divine revelation. It is more than whether or not we consider words like "according to Matthew" as the word of God. The fundamental problem is: What weight can such tradition carry in Christian teaching?

Christian authors are, understandably enough, reluctant to contradict what has been taught "always, everywhere, and by everyone." Nevertheless, even as early as the third century, Saint Cyprian, the bishop of Carthage, realized that if a tradition is not true then it is merely an old error. When a tradition, however widespread and venerable, proves to be wrong, then it should be recognized for what it is, an old error. Its perdurance through the ages can be blamed on nothing more complicated than just ordinary human reluctance to ask the right questions.

The defenders of such traditions of authorship will doubtless argue that the literary tools we have are not perfect and that our historical knowledge leaves much to be desired. This, of course, is quite true. Nevertheless, similar tools and less adequate knowledge have served all of us well in our investigation of other literary monuments of antiquity. The Bible, even as the word of God, is still a literary document; and, as such, it is not, and simply cannot be, exempt from the ordinary rules of literary composition. To exempt any literary composition from these rules would render them unintelligible to any ordinary human being.

Even for those who believe in the most direct divine intervention in the composition of our sacred books, the biblical authors could not have been just lifeless conduits for the divine message. Every human author leaves his own literary imprint on whatever he produces. The Bible as a literary document is subject to what we know about books and those who write them. If this were not so, then it would require more than human intelligence to make the Bible intelligible.

Now, among the distinctive qualities of any human author are what he says and the way he says it: content and style. Saint Paul mainfests such distinctive qualities in the letters we know are truly his, in Romans, in 1 Corinthians and the others. The Epistle to the Hebrews, on the other hand, even after the most concentrated search for its "Pauline" traits and even after the astutest interpretation of its theological content, refuses to fit into what we know of Paul's theology and style. Paul not only could not have written in the style of Hebrews, he did not think in its categories. And there need not be anything astonishing about any of this. To be a saint and an apostle cannot remove Paul from the ranks of mankind. When we say this we are simply saying that Paul was a human author and not a magician.

In the second example we mentioned above, that of 2 Peter, it is not only the title but also the text of the epistle that makes the claim of authorship for "Simon Peter, a servant and apostle of Jesus Christ" (2 Pet. 1:1). Yet, as we have had occasion to note in a previous chapter, it is precisely this epistle that makes reference to "our beloved brother Paul" and to "all his letters" (2 Pet. 3:15-16). If, as another constant and unrivaled tradition holds, Saint Peter was martyred in Rome around A.D. 64, during the reign of Nero, and if Saint Paul suffered the same fate shortly afterward (perhaps A.D. 67), no amount of historical fantasy and theological ingenuity can make the Second Epistle of Peter the work of "Simon Peter."

In this case, as in so many others, we simply have to accept the fact that in the ancient world the practice of writing under the name of a famous and revered person was not only common but perfectly acceptable. It was a popular form of literature, and even children in school were trained to acquire skill in writing a "letter of a famous person" much as they were trained to write an ode or an epigram.

But, even if we knew with certainty who wrote each of the books, we still would know very little about the authors themselves, not only of the New Testament, but of the whole Bible. Knowing the name of a certain author is no sure guarantee of knowing all that we ought to know about his person, his background, and his social situation. This, of course, complicates further the process of reading and understanding the books of our Bible.

The Primitive Christian Community

The problem of anonymity, however, extends beyond our New Testament into that earlier period when the traditions about Jesus were being formed and handed down orally. Within this context we have had occasion to speak of the "primitive Christian community." That community was credited with a lot of the work that went into the selection, formation and preservation of the traditions about Jesus.

Many have protested—and quite rightly—that a community is a rather sterile medium for the germination of ideas. It is indeed. Ideas and insights are begotten by individuals not by groups. Whatever is held by the many had to be held in the beginning by one. So, the argument continues, the primitive Christian community could not be credited with the work of shaping creatively the traditions about Jesus.

To argue this way is to miss the point behind the phrase "the primitive Christian community." This phrase is no more than a convenient formula for expressing the anonymity that veils those individual Christians who believed in Christ; and believing, reflected upon the meaning of their faith; and reflecting, arrived at those insights that proved so valuable in proclaiming to the world the good news of Jesus Christ.

Take, for instance, the various titles of Jesus in the New Testament. It has been estimated that there are fifty of them there: Lord, Son of God, Messiah, Son of Man, etc. These, evidently, were not a ready-made litany handed down from on high. They represent individual attempts to express who Jesus of Nazareth is, what he means and what he does.

No one pretends that these titles of Jesus were chosen by committee. When we attribute them to the primitive Christian community we are but admitting our ignorance of the identity of the Christian genius who first made the link, for example, between Jesus of Nazareth and Wisdom. Moreover, since these titles of Jesus have antecedents in the Old Testament, we are admitting our ignorance also of that still greater genius who first had the insight that the event of Jesus Christ is related to the entire Old Testament as fulfillment to promise.

Nevertheless, the community as such did have a role to play. As with the canonization of the books of the New Testament so too with the growth in understanding the significance of Jesus of Nazareth, the community of early Christians as a group was the fertile soil that accepted and nurtured those Christian ideas and insights. They had to experience the value of those links and connections and insights before they would accept them as expressions of their faith in Jesus Christ. They had to use them in their worship and preaching and missionary activity, and thus preserve them for future generations.

A "voice in the wilderness" is a figure of speech, no more. God's revelation is always addressed to a people, to a community. Revelation is a communal act. A prophet on the moon is no prophet at all. Moreover, God telling any prophet, "Go and tell this people . . .," was not and could not have been a one-way street. That people had to listen, to accept the word of the prophet, to recognize it as a divine message and respond to it as such. Otherwise, that word would be no more prophetic than any literary product of human genius.

Confronted by the people's rejection—the Bible calls it "disbelief"—even God is helpless. If the community ultimately refuses to accept an author as speaking God's message to them, no power could make that author's work "Sacred Scripture" for them. Without the realization of this basic fact, the Old Testament becomes unintelligible and the New Testament meaningless.

He came to his own home, and his own people received him not. But to all who received him, who believed in his name, he gave the power to become children of God (Jn. 1:11-12).

The freedom to accept or reject also belongs to the author. It is astonishing how many who are resolute defenders of the freedom of our act of faith think that, somehow, the sacred authors themselves had to be deprived of that freedom without which no faith can exist. An author of an Old or New Testament book could not have been an inanimate recorder. He had to believe in the God of the Fathers or in the Risen Lord worshiped by his people. But he had to believe in his own unique way, with his own mind and heart, and against his own individual background. He gave expression to that faith in the language of his day, with all the presuppositions of his world, and subject to the limitations of his own native ability, his own mastery of grammar and syntax, and his own imagination and literary creativity. The sacred author, in other words, was a flesh-and-blood individual whose vision, however sacred, was shaped and limited at every turn by the circumstances in which he lived and thought and wrote.

The people for whom the prophet or the apostle wrote had a decisive role to play too. It was ultimately they who accepted or rejected his message. If they rejected the work of someone as "non-canonical," if they refused to regard it as part of their sacred literature, that book could in no way be called the word of God for them. But, even before that happened, they had to listen to the author, judge him against the background of their own faith, and grant or refuse his work admission to their assemblies of worship. The believing community first accepted an author and then later— sometimes very much later—declared his work to be the word of God for them.

To that extent, therefore, the "primitive Christian community," despite its faceless anonymity, had an irreplaceable role to play. It was that community that first accepted to call Jesus the Wisdom of God, to read Paul's letters as Scriptures in their liturgical gatherings, and to accord the Gospels the reverence due to the word of God.

Needless to say, as the individual author's faith, presuppositions, background and prejudice necessarily mark a given book of the Bible, so too the believing community's faith, presuppositions, background and prejudice inevitably conditioned and determined what books got into the canon of the Bible and what books did not. In this way the anonymous "early Christian community" determined, shaped and conditioned our own understanding of who Jesus Christ is.

Therefore, our varying degrees of ignorance of those determinative factors, both for the individual authors and for the primitive Christian community, cannot but make us realize how very human our interpretation of the divine word has to be.

The Gospel Authors

Out of that faceless primitive Christian community there arose many individuals who, eager to preserve the oral traditions about Jesus and zealous to communicate his message to larger audiences, made the decision to set their precious memory down in writing. Although too few of us reflect on the profound change that takes place when a living word is immobilized into a written document, we cannot neglect to reflect upon the implications of this event in the history of our New Testament. We should try to understand that, when the words of Jesus finally came to be set down as "And he said to them . . .," something very decisive happened.

Because of the decision taken by that anonymous genius who first decided to collect and set down in writing the words of Jesus, which had hitherto been transmitted by word of mouth, a specific stage in the development of the Christian tradition was frozen in time. Naturally enough, that decision reflected the peculiar circumstances under which it took place. The language used was, in all likelihood, different from that in which the words were first uttered by Jesus of Nazareth. The background against which they were set down in writing was also quite different from the narrow geographic confines within which the ministry of Jesus was accomplished. But, above all, the purpose for which they were collected and set down was wholly different from that for which they were first spoken by Jesus. In collecting such sayings, of course, motives other than the simply chronological dictated the order and the arrangement.

As we saw above, such a document no longer exists. But its content, we surmise, served as a source (designated "Q") for documents of the first century which we do have today as the Gospels of Matthew and Luke. What we have to keep in mind, however, is that each of the two Gospels necessarily interpreted those sayings of Jesus in its own way. For no two people hear or read the same thing in exactly the same way; and the evangelists were no exception to this. To juxtapose two sayings is to invite understanding one in relation to the other. Thus the sayings of Jesus, in the very act of preservation and in their later use by the evangelists, underwent changes that are far from negligible.

Yet even if, for the sake of the argument, we were to suppose that the words of Jesus were set down in writing the moment he uttered them, and supposing they had been preserved in that mint condition and come down to us in that state, we would still be in difficulty. Beyond the translation from the language that Jesus spoke, which is certainly not ours, beyond understanding the conditions and the circumstances under which the words were uttered, we would still need to have those words interpreted. A human agency, in other words, would have to intervene to make those words intelligible to us. In this sense, Jesus does not speak to us directly in our Gospels.

In order to grasp the meaning and the nuance of the words spoken by Jesus, you need more than a knowledge of Aramaic and Greek, more than just accurate reporting and exactitude of details of how and when each word was uttered; you need some acquaintance with the geography, the social and religious institutions, the political and economic circumstances of first-century Palestine and the Roman world. Such knowledge is not normally communicated by divine inspiration and is rarely, if ever, exempt from error.

All these bits of necessary information are complicating human factors that, necessarily and inevitably, affect the meaning of the word of Jesus. None of them, however, can begin to compare with the factor introduced, willy nilly, by those who collected the sayings of Jesus and those who decided to include them in our four Gospels. Each of those individuals introduced personal and conditioned interpretations of the words of Jesus. They heard or read them, collected and selected them against individual backgrounds of beliefs, preferences and prejudices. Their act of writing too was addressed to a specific audience and solicited a certain response. The intended audience and the desired response also had roles to play in shaping the words of Jesus.

So, to lament the anonymity of the author of a Gospel is not to indulge a melancholy disposition. It does make a great deal of difference for our understanding of that Gospel if the author was in fact a Palestinian Jew, a tax collector for the hated Romans, and an apostle of Jesus who heard the private instructions of the Master and held sweet converse with him.

When such an author began to write his Gospel all these factors, and very many others besides, inevitably came into play. His attitude to the Jews, his attitude to the Romans, his attitude to the person of Jesus could not but color what he wrote. In other words, Matthew, whoever he really was, not only set down the tradition but also interpreted it. Indeed, by the time he came to write his Gospel, his own attitude to Jesus, to the Jews, and to the Romans had radically changed. So, having been a hearer of Jesus and an eye witness is no guarantee of delivering the words and deeds of his life in mint condition.

Being aware of all these difficulties does not diminish our ignorance; but it should mitigate it. Have we sufficiently reflected, for instance, on what effects the above factors could have on our understanding of Matthew 27:25 ("His blood be on us and our children!")? Yet these are not the words of Jesus but of a crowd such as we have grown accustomed to see in newspaper reports of riots and demonstrations. Even in reading such reports we instinctively seek to know whether the reporter was one of the rioters or not, a sympathetic observer or not, a native of that country or not, etc. Nevertheless, there have always been Christians ready to take Matthew's words at their face value, invest them with the authority of Sacred Scripture, and proceed to apply them in all the horrors of man's inhumanity.

But Matthew's account of Jesus' words and deeds is only one interpretation of at least four that we possess. Indeed, it is but one book out of twenty-seven that make up our New Testament. None of these can be studied in isolation. Before we turn to this particular aspect of the matter, however, we need to look at a stage in the progress of New Testament scholarship that takes us beyond Form Criticism and allied considerations.

Consequences of Form Criticism

It was the results of Form Criticism, mentioned in the previous chapter, which brought home the realization that: (1) our Gospels are made up of small individual units; and (2) the literary forms of these units have a history which reflects the situation in the life of the primitive Christian community.

Scholars went on to argue, however, that such traditions about Jesus as were contained in the individual units can only tell us what the primitive comunity believed and said about him, not what he himself said and believed about himself. So, scholars argued, we really cannot get at the Jesus of history, at what he actually said and did. All that we have in our New Testament, therefore, is the Christ in whom the primitive Christian community believed. That faith was necessarily refracted through the prism of their belief in the Resurrection of Jesus. Everything they said about him was, consequently, conditioned by their belief that Jesus of Nazareth had risen from the dead.

It was argued that the early Christian community was not interested—initially at least—in exactly what Jesus had said, precisely when he had performed a certain miracle, or just where he was when a certain event took place. They were not concerned about how he felt toward this or that situation. They were concerned rather to proclaim the Risen Christ, to explain what he means here and now to the community of the believers in him. They went forth to remind the Christians of the demands Christ makes of them now, the challenge he addresses to each of them individually. In other words, the first Christian missionaries and the early Christian communities were not interested in someone who had lived and died, but in the one who now lives and will die no more.

Consequently, it was argued, the evangelists too were not writing "biographies" of Jesus. They were rather Christians who collected what individual items of the tradition about Jesus were available to them and useful for the worship, the preaching, and the catechizing of their community. The links that the evangelists provided to join these bits and pieces of the transition together into one Gospel are not a part of that tradition. Such indications of time and place as we find in our Gospels are therefore incidental. They provide, as it were, the thread on which the traditions about the words and the deeds of Jesus are strung.

Thus, for example, when Mark 3 starts its various sections with "And when he returned to Capernaum . . ." (Mk. 3:1); "He went out again beside the sea . . ." (3:13); "And as he sat at table . . ." (3:15), etc., these indications need not all be accurate references to the time sequence or to the geographical location of the actual events in Jesus' life. Mark, the form critics insisted, was no more than a collector and editor of the various units in the tradition about Jesus.

There is much to be said for these observations of Form Criticism. But, as many scholars began to point out in the early fifties, there was one serious error that persisted in the form-critical assessment of our Gospels. It was pointed out that the authors of the Gospels were not and could not have been mere collectors of the traditions about Jesus. The evangelists, like those who transmitted the tradition orally before them, shaped and adapted that tradition to their own individual aims and purposes.

The evangelists, it was further argued against Form Criticism, had much more than record-keeping in mind. They were not archivists collecting and preserving every shred of evidence about the life and teaching of Jesus that they could find. They redacted, edited and shaped the material about Jesus. Each evangelist was therefore an author in the fullest sense of the term. The redaction and editing of the available material by each evangelist was, consequently, much more than stringing pearls on a string.

Redaction Criticism

Quite naturally, this further methodological step in the understanding of our Gospels was called Redaction Criticism. Redaction Criticism is concerned with what each evangelist, as an author in his own right, did when he collected, selected, ordered and shaped the various traditions about Jesus. It seeks to find out the ruling idea behind each Gospel and to see how each item, each individual pericope fits into the larger design of each of the four evangelists.

Thus, what each evangelist adds or subtracts—even if that be but a single word—in a given pericope can furnish us with some hint of his purpose in writing a gospel. The way each evangelist orders the material, whether geographically or chronologically, does matter a great deal. Consequently, the order of events in the life of Jesus, except in their broadest general outline, furnishes us with clues, not to the events themselves as they actually happened, but to the evangelist's conception of his work and the reason he had for writing a Gospel.

It is true that the evangelists made use of traditions about Jesus. But their use of them was creative. They had a message to bring to their readers and hearers. They did not set out to write a "life of Jesus." They used the literary device of recounting the life and teaching of Jesus in order to achieve something far more useful and compelling than just the inspiring biography of a great religious hero.

To grasp this point is to realize how each of our Gospels is, in its own individual way, an interpretation of what Jesus means to the believer in a Christian community. This is one valuable insight gained from Redaction Criticism. It should at least relieve us of the need to "harmonize" our four Gospels into one, to iron out the differences and discrepancies in their accounts, and to pretend that in any one of them we have an accurate, reliable, historical account of exactly what Jesus said and did. They are, to be sure, both accurate and reliable, but in relation to what each evangelist set out to do in them, not in compliance with our modern canons of historical accuracy.

Of course, it has been rightly pointed out that these Gospels are not just spinning out a tale about some religious hero created by the imagination of the early Christians. The center and object of the Gospels is a very real, very historical Jesus of Nazareth, who was born, lived, was crucified and died "under Pontius Pilate." Without this undeniable fact of history everything else in the Gospels would make absolutely no sense whatsoever.

Yet it would be to misunderstand and greatly depreciate the value of our Gospels were we to use them as quarries for material to construct a biography of Jesus. The response that the Gospels demand is not redoubled exertion in the field of archaeology, nor intensified research in ancient archives. They demand to be read not in order to provide us with a balance sheet of historical evidence, nor to compel us with irrefutable evidence about the words and deeds of a dead personage out of the distant past.

All this argument can perhaps be made clearer if we illustrate it by some examples from the Gospels themselves:

(1) The Baptism of Jesus. The Acts of the Apostles contain several summaries and sketches of what early Christian preaching about Jesus was like. In one such example (Acts 10:34-43) we have Peter saying:

> *"You know the word which [God] sent to Israel, preaching good news of peace by Jesus Christ . . . the word which was proclaimed throughout Judea, beginning from Galilee after the Baptism which John preached . . . " (Acts 10:36-37).*

This gives us some hint that, among the events of Jesus' life that were recalled in the early proclamation of the Christian message, the baptism was included as a starting point. It is, of course, the starting point of the public ministry of Jesus in all the four Gospels.

The first three Gospels provide us with accounts of the baptism of Jesus (Mt. 3:13-17; Mk. 1:9-11; Lk. 3:21-22). The accounts generally agree on what took place. But Matthew inserts into his narrative two verses (Mt. 3:14-15) to explain why Jesus came to John to be baptized at all. Evidently, Matthew had a good reason for including this explanation in his account.

By the time that Matthew came to write his Gospel, the baptism of Jesus was beginning to raise questions that simply did not cross the mind of the earlier generation of Christians. Evidently, believers in Matthew's time and within his community had begun to realize that if Jesus was truly sinless, then what was he doing getting baptized by John, who was preaching

> *a baptism of repentance for the forgiveness of sins (Mk. 1:4).*

Matthew tries to explain this in the verses he adds to his account of the baptism:

> *John would have prevented him, saying, "I need to be baptized by you, and do you come to me?" But Jesus answered him, "Let it be so now; for thus it is fitting for us to fulfil all righteousness" (Mt. 3:14-15).*

Moreover, in order to enhance the intelligibility of this enigmatic answer, he simply omits the mention of the baptism of John having been "for the forgiveness of sins" (Mk. 1:4).

Most ingenious explanations of these observable facts in the text of Matthew have been proposed. If you imagine the evangelist setting down a historical account accurate in every detail, then you will have to more than just explain. If, however, you see Matthew doing a specific job with a clear purpose in view, then you will have to ask what it is that Matthew, as distinct from Mark and Luke and John, is really trying to do. In recognizing that Matthew was more than merely transmitting intact certain traditions about Jesus, you obviate the necessity of ingenious explanations for the additions and omissions in Matthew's narrative.

(2) The Conditions of Discipleship. For the second example we can take the well-known saying of Jesus about "taking up the cross." This is found twice in Matthew (Mt. 10:38 and 16:24); once in Mark

(Mk. 8:34); and twice in Luke (Lk. 9:23 and 14:27). So the saying certainly has what is called multiple attestation, one of the norms for determining the words of Jesus that we examined in the previous chapter.

Let us suppose that Jesus did utter such a saying as:

"If any man would come after me, let him deny himself and take up his cross and follow me."

This is what Jesus says in Mark 8:34 and in Matthew 16:24; but this is decidely not what he says in Luke 9:23:

"If any man would come after me, let him deny himself and take up his cross daily *and follow me."*

To "take up the cross" and to take it up "daily" do not mean and cannot be made to mean the same thing. In Luke we have a figurative use of the phrase. What can be construed as a call to martyrdom in Matthew and in Mark is a call to asceticism in Luke. The former can be made to speak of death, the latter of abnegation and suffering. To try to reconcile the one with the other on the basis of historical accuracy and not with respect to the creative ingenuity of each evangelist is well-nigh impossible.

(3) The Our Father. Finally let us take up the example of the Our Father which was cited in the previous chapter. It simply cannot be by chance that Matthew included the prayer as part of Jesus' Sermon on the Mount while Luke sets it after the story of Martha and Mary (Lk. 10:38-42) as a response to the disciples' request, "Lord, teach us to pray!" (Lk. 11:1).

Apart from what we saw above about the differences in meaning between the two versions of the prayer, we have to realize that Matthew's view of how prayer fits into the Christian life is quite distinct from the place Luke assigns it. If we pay careful attention to what Luke does throughout his Gospel we will see that this particular instance of the Our Father fits well into his aim and purpose in writing.

The point of the example must be kept clearly in mind. What Luke is expressing in the Our Father is one understanding among several of Jesus' attitude to prayer. It is not easy—but perhaps possible—to reconcile this with the pictures presented by Mark, Matthew and

John. But such a reconciliation will yield a resultant portrait of Jesus and his attitude to prayer which is every bit as much an interpretation as any of its component parts. In other words, we would be substituting our own view for the individual views of four distinct evangelists.

What the evangelists set out to do was not to compile a history or compose a biography. Even Luke, for all the compelling force of his opening statement (Lk. 1:1-4), was satisfied that this was not so. What all the evangelists set out to do was to produce documents of faith. Their Gospels are calls to faith. But—and this is fundamental—they are calls to faith in a real, flesh-and-blood, historical person. Yet, it must be kept constantly in mind, the history of this person is subordinated to the faith and not the other way around. In other words, the authenticity of the Gospel accounts is the authenticity of the faith they call forth. It is not the accuracy of the narrative details the Gospels employ in order to call forth that faith.

Those who insist on regarding the Gospels as books of history will inevitably press their faith (particularly in the miraculous and the extraordinary) to explain away the glaring inconsistencies and the irreconcilable differences between them. Even the Gospel that most seems to go counter to this view with its protestations of telling nothing but the eyewitness truth about Jesus:

> *He who saw it has borne witness—his testimony is true, and*
> *he knows that he tells the truth—*

immediately adds,

> *that you also may believe (Jn. 19:35).*

To imagine this to be anything but religious faith is to miss the whole point, not of John's Gospel, but of all Christianity.

Review and Summary

The Gospels, as well as the other writings of the New Testament, are documents of faith. They are the product of faith, and are intended to call forth faith. They were written by individuals who believed in Jesus Christ and who tried to elicit a response of faith from their readers and hearers.

When the early Christian communities canonized these writings, they did so not for their reliability as historical documents, nor for the completeness of their record of Jesus of Nazareth. Those ultimately responsible for the inclusion of the twenty-seven books in our New Testament were neither antiquarians, nor scholars, nor librarians. They were Christian believers who judged these writings to be the word of God for them. They went out to proclaim their faith to the world and used these documents as explanations of the content and the implication of that faith.

There were many other books that recorded even more striking sayings of Jesus and more spectacular miracles. It was not for lack of credence in such documents that the Christians ultimately refused them admission to their canon of sacred books. The act of canonization was not so much a negative one of exclusion as a positive act of inclusion of certain books as good expressions of the faith the Christian community professed in Jesus Christ its Lord.

Of course, the process of selection was itself an interpretation on the part of the Christians. Their very choice of the books of the New Testament can tell us much about how the primitive community understood its faith in Jesus Christ. The canon of the New Testament is not a bibliography of early Christian theology. It is, in its own way, a theology: an act of interpretation of the meaning of the deeds accomplished by Jesus of Nazareth.

As the selection of the books themselves was an act of interpretation, so too was the selection of the material that went into them. Even that anonymous compiler of the sayings of Jesus, the author of "Q", exercised a choice and imposed an order. That choice necessarily reflected his own understanding of the meaning of Jesus Christ.

Similarly, Matthew's decision or Luke's to use that collection of sayings and incorporate it into their Gospels was an act of interpretation that depended as much on each evangelist's understanding of what faith in Jesus Christ meant as it did on his knowledge of the needs and preoccupations of the community to whom he wished to convey that meaning.

The evangelists, moreover, did not list haphazardly the various items they collected for their Gospels. They consciously selected them for their usefulness in conveying their own message. Form Criticism was indeed right to point out the fragmentary nature of our traditions about Jesus of Nazareth. Our Gospels are in fact made up of individual pericopes. But, as these pericopes had a history prior to their inclusion in the Gospels, they also have a history in each of the Gospels. Just as the form of these individual pericopes reflects the situation in the life of the Christian community that transmitted and shaped them, so too their present context in each Gospel reflects yet another situation in life: that of the community of believers for whom the Gospel was written.

All this is to say that, after carrying out the task of Form Criticism, we must take the added step of understanding what it is that each evangelist set out to do. The four Gospels are not carbon copies of each other. Therefore we need to explain, not only how, but also why they differ in their use of the same material about Jesus.

Moreover, even if the Evangelists were—as Form Criticism insisted they were—just collectors, the very ordering of their collection was an act of personal interpretation, a creative act. The order into which they arranged the material would, in itself, require explanation. This explanation is what Redaction Criticism tries to offer.

Thus, Redaction Criticism insists that the evangelists were creative authors and not just mechanical compilers. Consequently, an effort has to be made to discover the creative genius at work in each of the Gospels. Each has to be seen as an act of interpretation of the meaning of Jesus Christ for a specific community by a highly original and creative Christian thinker. In other words, the four evangelists have to be regarded as among the first Christian theologians.

The first believers in Jesus and our own contemporaries in the faith are no different in this. Everyone's understanding of the significance of Jesus Christ is necessarily subject to personal factors of background, need, preference and prejudice. The distance of twenty centuries does not put us or the theologians in our midst at a disadvantage. What sets the four evangelists in a place apart from all that followed them is not the accuracy of their portraiture but the relevance of their faith for us as a Christian community.

That relevance is ultimately responsible for the early Christians' choice of these four Gospels over all others. Their accounts of what Jesus said and did remain for all that interpretations, even if we choose to insist that they were divinely inspired interpretations. Our faith in them as the word of God to us, however, does not absolve us from the need to understand their true nature as literary documents.

Faith is not license for facile interpretation, and religious zeal is no substitute for hard work.

The temptation to produce a unified description of the person of Jesus from the four accounts might be understandable; but, in the final analysis, it is futile. Yielding to such a temptation can only produce a "Jesus of the imagination." To achieve a unified description of Jesus you need either to suppress whole sections of our Gospels to end up with a caricature, or to insist on including every detail to end up in an incredible contradiction.

What usually happens in such an undertaking is that a selection out of the four Gospels is made. And, however impartial we might try to be, that selection is ultimately dictated by one's own set of preferences and prejudices. It can only yield a Jesus of the imagination, a construct of what I happen to believe the finest specimen of humanity should be like, feel like and think like.

Such an exercise might be exhilarating in conception, but it is tyranny in its execution. The desire to enter into the mind and heart of so beloved a person as Jesus, to know what he liked and what he disliked, what views he held on this topic or that, is all too understandable. What renders it suspect is the end to which it inevitably leads. For we who indulge in such an exercise are people who believe that Jesus is God, his words are the words of God for us, his commands and wishes the norm and rule of our lives. Having completed our portrait of him, and having bolstered it up with appropriate texts from the four Gospels, we cannot but impose this Jesus on ourselves and on our fellow Christians as the ultimate law of Christian life and conduct. Thus, what started out as an innocent exercise of the imagination ends up as a tool of subjugation. Good intentions here count for naught. Twenty centuries of Christian history furnish us with ample evidence of the danger such a Jesus of the imagination can be.

Redaction Criticism can, I believe, serve as a corrective to such a tendency. It should keep before our eyes the nature of our Gospels and of the traditions on which they rest. Because, no matter what view of divine revelation we choose to espouse, there is no getting around the highly individual factor of human interpretation, even of the word of God. Had Jesus addressed each individual evangelist personally, that evangelist would still have had to interpret what he heard. Like it or not, he will have had to interpret it in his own unique way.

The early Christian communities must have known, at least instinctively, the risk that all personal interpretation runs. Their selection of *four* Gospels was the way they avoided that risk. That act of canonization ultimately said that the Christian communities recognized these four interpretations of the traditions about Jesus as "sacred." They were the word of God to them.

Shortly after the four Gospels began to acquire their place of honor among the Christian communities, someone in the church had the idea of combining all four and reducing them to one single Gospel, which is known as the *Diatessaron* of Tatian. Tatian's work met with great and long-lived success in a good many Christian communities. The church at large, however, fought against it and, in the end, won out with its four Gospels—four very different Gospels.

Every attempt to produce a unified portrait of Jesus' life and teachings is but a repetition of Tatian's folly. The inexhaustible riches of the person of Jesus Christ lie not in the harmonization of the New Testament books but in their uniqueness and diversity. If Jesus Christ is truly who we say he is, then no one Gospel, no one book of the New Testament, can comprehend all that faith in him signifies.

4   The Good News of Mark

If the church was eager to preserve the uniqueness and distinctive character of each of the four Gospels, then in the Gospel of Mark it preserved the archetype of all their originality. The centuries of reverent neglect which Mark suffered in the Christian churches has been more than vindicated in recent times. It was quite understandable that a church, which believed Mark to be merely derivative, a condensation of the Gospel of Matthew, should turn to the latter for the lessons in its liturgy, the texts of its sermons, and the arguments for its theology.

If practically all of Mark can be found in Matthew and Luke, then what need was there to go to it at all? The few items that are peculiar to Mark's Gospel seemed to ill serve the theology and piety of the church. Even when the nineteenth century "rediscovered" Mark it was for what most today would judge the wrong reasons. Mark was valued as the most "historical" of the Gospels, preserving the most accurate order of events, and transmitting the tradition about Jesus in its pristine integrity. But the true originality and distinctiveness of Mark must be sought elsewhere.

With the arrival of Redaction Criticism on the scene in the early 1950s the Gospel of Mark truly came into its own. It did so, not because of the hypothesis of its priority over both Matthew and Luke, nor because of the chronological value of its order of events, and certainly not because of its weight as historical evidence for the life of Jesus. Mark's Gospel came into its own because New Testament scholars realized the astounding genius of an author who produced a Christian document without any known antecedent in previous literature and with but very few successful imitations since. It was a genius which, out of the largely undifferentiated mass of the available oral—and perhaps also written—traditions, called forth a new creation that he entitled "the gospel of Jesus Christ."

The problem of the anonymity of this genius, one of the most creative minds in the history of Christian theology, weighs heavily against our full assessment of his achievement. There is, it is true, an ancient tradition reported by a fourth-century ecclesiastical historian, Eusebius of Caesarea, and going back to Papias, the bishop of Jerusalem in the first half of the second century. This tradition maintains that, though Mark had neither heard nor followed the Lord, he was an "interpreter" of Saint Peter. He remembered and wrote down, fully and faithfully, what he had thus heard from the great apostle.

Whatever of this old tradition we wish to accept, the person called Mark remains unknown to us. Even if we allow the accuracy of the report in Eusebius, our most urgent questions remain unanswered: What made this Mark write this particular kind of literary composition? What lay behind his selection and ordering of the material that was at his disposal? What motivated his undertaking? etc. Mere biographical tidbits about Mark will answer none of these questions adequately.

Approaches to Mark

The data about our Synoptic Gospels, to which we referred above, leave most modern scholars convinced that Mark was the first Gospel ever written. Such data convince most scholars today that Matthew and Luke depended on Mark as a source in the composition of their own Gospels. So, while we can compare Matthew and Luke with each other and with Mark to see how each used, altered and adapted his material, we really have nothing with which to compare Mark himself. All attempts to find a model for Mark inside or outside Christianity have failed. We do not even know whether he was following any literary model known to him. Thus, to the problem of the anonymity of its author is added the difficulty of the uniqueness of his Gospel.

Nevertheless, in order to understand the Gospel of Mark, we must have some answer to the questions about the purpose, the motive and the rationale behind the selectivity in it. We are compelled, especially in the case of this Gospel, to call upon all the tools and insights of literary criticism that are available to us. For after a careful and attentive reading of the text of Mark, we have to ask: What was that "fundamental intuition of form" that enabled the author to assemble all the disparate elements of the traditions about Jesus into a coherent and unified whole?

The Gospel of Mark has to be read at one go, from start to finish. Only this way will we get some hint of the larger undertaking, some appreciation of the vision that shaped it, and some idea of the compelling challenge it addresses to its readers. Such a reading of this or any other Gospel will compel us to ask what it is that we really have in this literary composition; what its author was trying to do in narrating a sequence of events about Jesus of Nazareth.

In the Gospel of Mark we are at a definite stage in the interpretation of who Jesus of Nazareth is; we are at one privileged moment—now forever fixed in writing—in the history of Christian theology. The oral traditions, as we saw above, underwent their own transformation and adaptation to the needs—liturgical, catechetical, polemical, etc.—of the community. Those traditions were being interpreted by the Christian preachers and missionaries who proclaimed that the Jesus they preached was living and active in their midst. They were not handing on edifying anecdotes and inspiring sayings, but addressing a challenge and calling for a response in faith. The author of Mark was one of those preachers. His distinction is that he left a written record behind him.

Indeed, all four Gospels are no less challenges. They are four interpretations of the person and the work of Jesus. It is for this that they occupy such a privileged place in our Bible. But their worth as interpretations did not derive from the privilege that was conferred upon them by including them in the canon of Sacred Scripture. Rather it was the other way around. Christian believers first saw in the Gospels compositions of inestimable worth as interpretations of who Jesus is and what he means, and only then did they accord them the respect and the veneration that ultimately led to their canonization as "the word of God."

The Beginning

So now we come to the first of the attempts to gather together into a consecutive narrative, and to interpret as a coherent unit, the traditions about the words and deeds of Jesus of Nazareth. If Mark followed a prior model, that model is not known to us. If, as some maintain, his work was originally in a different form, that form is now not available to us. What we do have is a composition called the Gospel according to Mark, whose opening words read:

The beginning of the gospel of Jesus Christ, the Son of God.

It is with this document that we have to deal.

That "beginning," it has been pointed out, is in fact a threefold beginning. It is, first of all, the beginning of a series of events, leading from the baptism of Jesus to his passion and crucifixion. This series of events forms, as it were, the skeletal structure of the two other Synoptics as well. In Mark it is a series of events that follow one another in rapid succession:

> *John the baptizer appeared in the wilderness. . . . In those days Jesus came from Nazareth of Galilee. . . . The Spirit immediately drove him out into the wilderness. . . . Now after John was arrested. . . . And passing along by the Sea of Galilee. . . .*

All this between verses 4 and 16 of the first chapter of the Gospel.

The events in Mark are rarely interrupted by lengthy discourses as they are in Matthew and Luke. They move quite rapidly toward the Passion, which occupies a very sizable part in all the Gospels. This fact prompted someone to remark that our Gospels are rather like lengthy introductions to the Passion. This remark, as we shall see, is particularly apt for the Gospel of Mark.

Thus, starting with the appearance of John on the scene, Mark narrates a succession of events in the life of Jesus of Nazareth. So there is good reason to consider the "beginning" in Mark 1:1 as referring to a series of events that lead to the passion and crucifixion of Jesus.

It is, secondly, the "beginning" of the act of writing. What had hitherto survived in the disparate oral fragments of folk memory was to be set down in writing. It is, of course, more than merely a classical proverb that the written word "abides," is fixed and will not be effaced from the memory. Mark's act of setting down those traditions in the language of a people in the first century was thus a "beginning."

Even if some of the traditions existed in some written form and were available to Mark in that form, his inclusion of them in his Gospel also marked the beginning of a new use and purpose. The purposes such traditions once served were now taken up and reformulated by an author setting out on an entirely new course.

That beginning of the act of writing by an author we call Mark left, even if indirectly, the stamp of his understanding and interpretation of Jesus Christ on the mind of Christianity forever.

Thirdly, the "beginning" is, as the Gospel clearly states:

> *The beginning of the gospel of Jesus Christ, the Son of God.*

Now "gospel" comes from the Old English *gōd,* meaning good, and *spel,* meaning news or tidings. It translates well the Latin *evangelium,* which is a literal rendition of the Greek *euangelion,* meaning good news. From that same root, of course, we have such words as "evangelist" and "evangelical."

To anyone reading these opening words of Mark's Gospel, the good news is: (1) The fulfillment of the prophecy,

> *"Behold, I send my messenger before thy face, who shall prepare thy way. . ." (Mk. 1-2),*

in the person and the ministry of John the Baptist, who

> *appeared in the wilderness, preaching a baptism of repentance for the forgiveness of sins (Mk. 1:4).*

(2) The message taught by Jesus Christ throughout the Gospel. Indeed, Mark reserves the use of the verb "to teach" exclusively to Jesus.

(3) The good news concerning Jesus Christ. This is what is being proclaimed in every page of Mark. By calling his work a "gospel" in this sense, the author created a new category of literature that was distinctively Christian. It was the kind of composition that, as far as we know, was wholly original with him.

This is not to say that the author of Mark coined the word "gospel." He did not. Saint Paul knew and used it before him with reference to the good news concerning Jesus Christ. Paul speaks of himself as "an apostle, set apart for the gospel of God" (Rom. 1:1), and as sent by Christ "to preach the gospel" (1 Cor. 1:17). But what sets Mark apart is the form he gave that mode of declaring the good news of Jesus Christ: the arrangement of a series of events leading from the baptism of Jesus to the Passion, the account of the teaching and the miracles of Jesus, and that long and unsparing account of his suffering and death.

In order to appreciate the true worth of this truly original contribution to Christian theology, we must try to find out the governing idea of the work, what is usually called "the mind of the author." But, as in all truly impressive works of human genius, this is not an easy task, nor as simple as the rest of this chapter might make it appear.

The Framework of Mark

Our principal means of access to this "mind of the author," to the ruling idea that governed his work, is the framework of his Gospel. It is not merely the content, the words and deeds of Jesus, that will enable us to grasp the significance of the Gospel of Mark. Most of this material was already available in the oral—and perhaps also written—traditions utilized by the author. So we must find out what it is that Mark did with that available material. Therein lies the clue to his genius. It is what he selected and, above all, how he arranged the traditions that were available to the Christians of his generation that constitute his particular contribution. Thus it is that the framework of his Gospel might eventually enable us to apprehend the meaning of "the good news of Jesus Christ" according to Mark.

Even a cursory reading of Mark will reveal a broad geographical outline. It charts the progress of the ministry of Jesus:

from Galilee (Mk. 1:14-6:13), beyond Galilee (Mk. 6:14-8:26), from Caesarea Philippi to Jerusalem (Mk. 8:27—10:52), and in Jerusalem itself (Mk. 11:1—16:8).

We should be careful to note here that the Gospel of Mark, as it has come down to us, ends at Mark 16:8. The verses that follow, verses 9-20, are later additions by people who obviously did not think a gospel could or should end with the words:

And they went out and fled from the tomb; for trembling and astonishment had come upon them; and they said nothing to any one, for they were afraid.

Thus, the Gospel of Mark, unlike the other three, does not end with the accounts of the appearances of the Risen Jesus to his disciples.

Now, within the progress of Jesus' ministry from one region of Palestine to another, there appear, upon closer inspection of the text of the Gospel, further divisions. These breaks in the narrative contain summary statements like:

> *And he went throughout all Galilee, preaching in their synagogues and casting out demons (Mk. 1:39; see also 2:13; 10:1, etc.).*

If we remember that our New Testament texts, like the texts of antiquity, were written without many of the conventions to which our books have accustomed us (chapter headings, paragraph indentation, even the separation of one word from another), then such devices as the summaries in Mark become more comprehensible. They are, as in all good literary compositions, aids to transition from one idea to the next. At the same time they serve as means of accentuating the essential points of the argument. But, of themselves, they are insufficient to convey the author's message. The rivets in a structure, the seams in a dress do not tell the whole story. They are indicators at best.

The whole framework of the Gospel must be grasped in order to allow us to see the relations of the parts to each other and, above all, their function within the whole. A work as original as Mark's Gospel has had, quite naturally, more than its share of theories to explain these structural relationships. Not all such theories are equally convincing; nor are they necessarily mutually exclusive. Each, in its own way, can be an aid to a better understanding of the mind of the author of Mark.

Of course, these theories remain human attempts at interpreting a literary creation of great originality. They are more or less successful, always open to improvement and subject to modification. No one interpretation can lay claim to being exclusively inspired. No church has "defined" the meaning of any Gospel. So every theory is only as good as the reasons it proposes and the premises upon which its argument rests.

This, however, need not surprise or disconcert even the most ardent believer that Mark's Gospel is the word of God. If Mark is the word of God, then it should at least enjoy the complexity of interpretations that the great works of human genius call forth from every generation. When was the last time you saw a "definitive interpretation" of an epic of Homer, an ode of Horace, a play of Shakespeare, or an Andersen fairy tale? To want to exempt God's word from such diversity of interpretations is not to do it honor but to reduce it to the inanities of billboard advertising.

The Messianic Secret

Even before Form Criticism made its appearance on the New Testament scene and insisted—a bit too one-sidedly, as has been suggested—on the quality of the evangelists as collectors of traditions, it was noted that the author of Mark had introduced into his collection a theme that is peculiar to him. That theme was identified as "the messianic secret."

Very briefly, this theory maintained that the evangelist had introduced into his material a motif of secrecy. Jesus, for instance, "would not permit the demons to speak, because they knew him" (Mk. 1:34); he "strictly charged" the people who witnessed the raising of the ruler's daughter to life that "no one should know this" (Mk. 5:43); and, in response to Peter's confession of "You are the Christ," he gave an order "to tell no one about him" (Mk. 8:30).

The proponents of this theory maintained that Mark himself introduced this motif of secrecy in response to a specific need within his community. It might have been introduced, for example, to explain the failure of Jesus' contemporaries to recognize and acknowledge who he really was. It might have been introduced to explain how the true identity of Jesus had to remain concealed "until the Son of Man should have risen from the dead" (Mk. 9:9).

But, whatever the reasons for the presence of this secrecy motif in the Gospel of Mark, it was argued that it was a contribution of the author himself to the material already available to him. In other words, Mark was acting as more than just a collector and recorder of traditions. He was interpreting and modifying that material with a specific purpose in mind.

Nevertheless, as often happens, other scholars came along and pointed out that the secrecy motif is really not very consistent throughout the Gospel of Mark. Even if Jesus enjoined secrecy on his followers, "privately to his own disciples he explained everything" (Mk. 4:34). Commands like "tell no one" seemed to have been more like invitations to disobedience:

> *But the more he charged them, the more zealously they proclaimed it (Mk. 7:36).*

Moreover, after Peter's confession in Mark 8:29 and the subsequent command "to tell no one about him" (Mk. 8:30), Jesus goes on to divulge the secret quite plainly and without mincing his words (Mk. 8:31-32).

What takes place after Peter's confession, however, is far more interesting than the command to secrecy. The disciples of Jesus, who hitherto had trouble understanding who he was and what he was talking about, begin to misunderstand him completely.

The Disciples in Mark

This strange phenomenon has led some recent scholars to propose a structure of Mark based, more or less, on the response of the disciples to Jesus. In this theory, the structure of Mark would be along the following lines:

(1) From the beginning of the Gospel and up to Mark 8:27, Peter's confession, the disciples show themselves incredibly obtuse and imperceptive:

> *"Do you not understand this parable?" (Mk. 4:13); "Have you no faith?" (4:40); "Do you not yet perceive or understand? Are your hearts hardened? Having eyes do you not see, and having ears do you not hear? And do you not remember?" (8:18).*

All these remonstrations of Jesus with his disciples are pretty devastating to their reputations.

Of course, Peter's confession at Caesarea Philippi seemed to change all that. It revealed, or seemed to reveal, a high degree of understanding. To Jesus' question:

> *"But who do you say I am?"*

the apostle gave the perfectly correct answer:

> *"You are the Christ" (Mk. 8:29).*

(2) Yet, from that moment on to the beginning of the Passion, to Mark 14:9, Peter himself and all the disciples with him show that

they really misunderstood Jesus. True, Peter had confessed him to be the Christ, the Messiah, the anointed one (for that is what the Greek *Christos* translates from the Hebrew *Messiah,* which means "anointed"). But Peter and the rest completely misunderstood the true meaning of this messiahship. Their initial lack of understanding had now given way to a gross misconception of what the Christ was all about.

For, as soon as Jesus introduces the talk of suffering, Peter begins to "rebuke him" (Mk. 8:32). When Jesus tells the disciples of the kingdom they begin to jostle for precedence (9:34) and dream of preferment (10:37). They believe Jesus is the Messiah, but quite a different Messiah from the suffering Messiah he foretold.

(3) Finally, the misunderstanding of the disciples turns to out-and-out betrayal and rejection. From Judas' betrayal:

> *Then Judas Iscariot, who was one of the twelve, went to the chief priests in order to betray him to them (Mk. 14:10);*

to the abandonment by the disciples:

> *And they all forsook him, and fled (14:15);*

to the sworn denial by Peter himself:

> *But he began to invoke a curse on himself and to swear, "I do not know this man" (14:71).*

Such a view of the Gospel of Mark finds in all this a "carefully formulated polemical device created by the evangelist to disgrace and debunk the disciples." The reason the proponents of such a view give is that, at the time that Mark wrote his Gospel, there was a debate raging within the Christian community. The debate centered on whether Jesus was the Messiah in the sense of a triumphant, miracle-working hero; or whether he was a suffering, crucified Messiah.

According to this view, the disciples (i.e., all the followers of Jesus) who grossly misunderstand who Jesus really is and what his miracles signify, inevitably end up by refusing to follow him. In other words, the Gospel reflects a debate within the Christian community about the true answer to be given to "Who do you say I am?" The community of Mark was split over whether the answer was to be a triumphant Christ or a suffering Messiah.

That such a debate could have divided the Christian community is not surprising. It is a debate that continues right into the present, even if its terminology has changed. That such a debate should find echoes in the Gospel of Mark is not implausible. But what makes the theory about the disciples' deteriorating position in Mark questionable is that the failure of the disciples, even if very real, is neither total nor complete. Mark's Gospel does not end with Peter's denial. Its story continues and goes on to tell of the young man's message to the woman at the empty tomb:

> *"Go tell his disciples* and Peter *that he is going before you to Galilee; there you will see him, as he told you" (Mk. 16:7).*

Had the failure of the disciples been total, the Gospel could hardly have been "the good news of Jesus Christ" to anybody in the first or the twentieth century. Whatever else it might be, Mark's message is clearly one of hope. It is truly "good news" to all the disciples, past and present, who have known failure and have "broken down and wept" (Mk. 14:72) for their betrayal.

Discipleship in Mark

In this approach to Mark's Gospel, as in almost any other that has been proposed, one thing keeps emerging persistently. There is no doubt that the disciples of Jesus have a decisive role to play throughout the Gospel. They are, so to speak, one of the principal means employed by the author to give sequence and continuity to the disparate units of the tradition about Jesus. But they are also clearly there to instruct Mark's readers, whether in his community or in ours. They are the ones with whom, to use the current idiom, the reader identifies. Jesus' questions to the disciples are addressed to the readers, his instructions to the disciples are meant for them. Thus, the whole Gospel of Mark can be seen as an instruction on discipleship, on what it means to believe in and be a follower of Jesus Christ.

The Gospel of Mark, then, can be regarded as an attempt to explain the true meaning of Jesus Christ to the believers within a Christian community some forty or fifty years after his death. But the explanation of what we mean when we confess that "Jesus is the Christ" is not an intellectual exercise. Mark realizes, as do all the New Testament authors, that belief in Christ is not just a conviction,

"You are the Christ!," but a life. It is a life of following in the way of a crucified Lord:

> *"If any man would come after me, let him deny himself and take up his cross and follow me" (Mk. 8:34).*

So, whatever ruling insight we might discern in the structuring of Mark's Gospel must, in some way or another, be oriented to the Passion. The Passion not only occupies a substantial part of the text of the Gospel but dominates the unfolding of all the events. There are pointers to it interspersed throughout the account of Jesus' ministry. As early as Mark 3:6 we read:

> *The Pharisees went out, and immediately held counsel with the Herodians against him, how to destroy him.*

But there is a whole series of such pointers to the Passion clustered around the turning point of the narrative: Peter's confession at Caesarea Philippi (Mk. 8:27-30).

A close study of these passages has yielded a pattern which provides us with one major clue to understanding what the author of Mark set out to do. For, immediately after the high point in Jesus' public ministry, when Peter confesses him to be "the Christ" (Mk. 8:29), the author adds,

> *And he began to teach them that the Son of man must suffer many things, and be rejected by the elders and the chief priests and the scribes, and be killed, and after three days rise again (Mk. 8:31).*

But, no sooner had Jesus spoken "plainly" to his disciples, when the very same Peter, who had just acknowledged him to be the Christ, began to object to this wholly unacceptable image of the Messiah. He had, quite evidently, completely misunderstood the kind of Christ this Jesus was.

Jesus' rebuke of Peter is harsh but to the point:

> *"Get behind me, Satan! For you are not on the side of God, but of men" (Mk. 8:33).*

Not even the praise for Peter that Matthew includes in anticipation of this rebuke in his account: "For flesh and blood have not revealed this to you, but my Father who is in heaven" (Mt. 16:17), can really soften the words of Jesus. Any way you choose to interpret it, Mark's view of the whole incident is quite clear. To expect a triumphant Messiah, one with guaranteed success and overwhelming victory, is to be "not on the side of God."

Now, to try to put this incident back into Jesus' life is to miss its whole point. As an incident in Jesus' life it is just a past news item. As an account in Mark's Gospel it becomes a present challenge. When Mark wrote these lines he and his community believed in the Risen Lord as much as we do. Mark was, even at that early stage, warning against the triumphalistic image of Jesus that is as tempting to Christians today as it was two thousand years ago.

At this point one might have expected Mark to show Jesus delivering a proper corrective to Peter's view of the Messiah. But Jesus does not correct Peter's misunderstanding by explaining what the true nature of the Christ is but by describing what a true Christian disciple should be. In other words, the truest confession of faith in Jesus receives its worth and meaning from the life of the believer, not from the dogma within which it is formulated. To confess Jesus as the Christ is not a theological undertaking but a commitment. It is an option to follow Jesus. How?

> *"If any man would come after me, let him deny himself and take up his cross and follow me" (Mk. 8:34).*

The curious thing in Mark's Gospel, however, is that this pattern is repeated three times: a prediction of the Passion, followed by a misunderstanding by the disciples, followed by an instruction on discipleship. The third time culminates with what is very clearly a focal point of the whole Gospel of Mark.

Thus, after the second prediction of the Passion (Mk. 9:31), Mark not only tells us:

> *But they did not understand the saying (9:32),*

but goes on to illustrate the misunderstanding. The disciples start discussing "with one another who was the greatest" (9:34). Once again, Jesus corrects the misunderstanding not by a discourse on the Messiah but by an instruction on discipleship, on what it means to be a true follower of Jesus Christ:

*"If any one would be first, he must be last of all and servant
of all" (9:35).*

It never ceases to amaze any student of Christian history how
often those who are "first" are prone to espouse the loftiest concep-
tions of Jesus of Nazareth. Theirs is always the truth before which all
else is error to be banished. Theirs is a theology that knows no
setbacks, but only progress from one triumph of dogma to the next.
Mark shows the disciples of Jesus to have been no exception to this
very human tendency to use dogma for dominance. The Jesus of
Mark challenges them and us to a total reversal of that tendency:
"the first . . . must be last of all."

Whether Mark ever thought of all these implications or not, it is
impossible to tell. What is unmistakable in this section of his Gospel,
however, is the intimate connection he stresses between Christian
confession and Christian life. The disciples' confession of the Christ
is awry because their action as Christians is dead wrong. Their error
is not so much in the confession of Jesus as in their ambition to have
the first places; and not so much in the ambition itself as in the
shirking of service: ". . . and servant of all" (Mk. 9:35).

The third series of prediction-misunderstanding-discipleship in the
Gospel of Mark becomes even more explicit on this point and
climaxes in one of the most concise responses given by the entire
New Testament to "Who do you say I am?"

The third prediction of the Passion is more explicit and detailed
than the first two. It adds to them,

they will mock him, and spit upon him (Mk. 10:34).

The misunderstanding that follows is more elaborately portrayed
too. Two of the disciples come to plead for high places of honor "in
your glory" (Mk. 10:35-40). This gross misunderstanding of Jesus'
messiahship is countered by a third instruction of discipleship that is
a quite unexpected synthesis of the first two.

Whereas in the first instruction discipleship was defined by suffering, "take up his cross" (Mk. 8:34); and in the second by service,
"last of all and servant of all" (9:35); the third combines both into:

*"Whoever would be great among you must be your servant,
and whoever would be first among you must be slave of all.*

For the Son of man came not to be served but to serve, and
to give his life as a ransom for many" (Mk. 10:43-45).

To confess Jesus as the Christ is to be his disciple, to follow him. To be his disciple means to be servant of all and slave to all. But this service inevitably entails suffering. That is why the "deny himself" is linked to "take up his cross and follow me" (Mk. 8:34). And the way to follow him is: the Passion of Jesus Christ according to Mark.

No reader of Mark's Passion can avoid being struck by the realism of the sufferings and the horror of the details. Indeed, the evangelists who followed Mark felt the need to suppress the more painful and less acceptable features in the account. Mark's gaze on the Christ is unblinking. He alone records Jesus'

"My God, my God, why hast thou forsaken me?" (Mk.
15:34).

For the reader of Mark's Gospel no amount of Easter allelujas will suffice to relieve him of the arduous necessity to serve, to take up the inevitable cross, and to follow the crucified Lord.

There are perhaps loftier visions of Christianity than Mark's; but there is no more demanding conception of the true Christian. Only those believers who genuinely seek to serve will understand why it was not irony but realism that prompted Mark to call his work,

the good news of Jesus Christ.

5   The Book of Matthew

Whether or not "book" describes best the work commonly attributed to Matthew, this is the word with which he opens his Gospel. It
is, as we have already seen, a work that is based essentially on two
sources: the Gospel of Mark and "Q." The fact that Mark's work
was utilized at all for so short a time—perhaps only about ten years—
after its appearance is some indication of the success it must have
enjoyed in the Christian communities, a success that must have
brought it to the attention of two other authors, Matthew and Luke,
who made a similar decision to write a Gospel.

That Matthew had Mark's original plan to follow does not, of
course, diminish the magnitude of his own achievement. He was not
merely someone who expanded the initial Markan framework to
incorporate into it the contents of "Q" as well as other pieces of
tradition that he judged useful to include. It was his own individual
vision that shaped the whole book into a document that responded to
the needs of his readers and gave a unique expression to their faith in
Christ Jesus.

The additional pieces of tradition that Matthew incorporated into
the material already available to him in Mark and "Q" are part of
that oral legacy about Jesus which none of our canonical Gospels
exhausts. The fact that Matthew uses the ones he does is simply
indicative of their popularity within his own circles. They account
for those events and sayings recounted by Matthew and by no one
else. They constitute most of the material prior to the Baptism of
Jesus as well as most of the Old Testament texts that are so frequently cited in his Gospel. It is these additions that give Matthew's
Gospel its special and characteristic features.

This added material, however, was not the only means employed by Matthew to achieve his purpose. He improved Mark's Greek, which stood in need of improvement; he shortened Mark's narratives by omitting the concrete details of which Mark was fond; and he systematized much of the material available to him elsewhere in the tradition.

The clearly observable fact of Matthew's shortening of the different narratives in Mark is quite remarkable. Tradition maintained for centuries that it was Mark who actually "abbreviated" Matthew. Saint Augustine, who is largely responsible for the popularity of that tradition, could easily have been spared the false conclusion had he but had a synopsis of the Gospels with which to work.

A look at any synopsis comparing Matthew and Mark will show that the latter's is, almost invariably, the longer text and the one with greater details. Matthew's much longer Gospel is due, of course, to the addition of "Q" and other material. But Matthew's elimination of many of the concrete details in Mark was not just an economy measure. It really achieved a greater concentration of attention on the person of Jesus. Since most of this material has to do with Mark's accounts of the miracles of Jesus, Matthew also succeeds in conveying, through this economy of details, the absolute indispensability of faith in this context.

This will become clearer if we compare, for instance, the conclusion of the incident involving the woman who pleaded with Jesus to heal her possessed daughter. Jesus' rather gratuitous and harsh response calls forth from the woman a profession of her faith in him. Mark concludes the narrative thus:

> *And he said to her, "For this saying you may go your way; the demon has left your daughter." And she went home, and found the child lying in bed, and the demon gone (Mk. 7:29-30).*

Now compare Matthew's conclusion of the same incident:

> *Then Jesus answered, "O woman, great is your faith! Be it done for you as you desire." And her daughter was healed instantly (Mt. 15:28).*

The economy of the conclusion concentrates the reader's attention both on the great faith of the woman and on Jesus' power.

On the other hand, Matthew's systematizing of the other traditions available to him took many forms. He grouped the words of Jesus according to subject. Thus, for example, within the Sermon on the Mount, he gathered material on religious practices together: on almsgiving, on prayer (including the Our Father), and on fasting in 6:1-18).

Other schematic arrangements within the Gospel can also be found easily. There are, for instance, seven parables in chapter 13; ten miracles are strung together in chapters 8 and 9. Such tendencies in the author led many to believe that the principal parts of the Gospel are also schematically arranged according to some significant number. Whether or not they are, there is no avoiding the fact that Matthew introduced order where there was none and arranged the available material into a larger and more coherent design.

The Structure of Matthew

One of the most remarkable features of Matthew's Gospel is the use he makes of the Old Testament. About half the material found in Matthew has no parallel in Mark. Much of this added material (about five-ninths of it) does have a parallel in Luke. This is usually assigned to "Q" as a source. What remains is material that is peculiar to Matthew. Much of this material consists of allusions or actual quotations from some 130 Old Testament passages.

Such quotations in Matthew bear their own identification mark:

> *All this took place to fulfil what the Lord had spoken by the prophet (Mt. 1:22);*
> *For it is written by the prophet (Mt. 2:5);*
> *That what was spoken by the prophet Isaiah might be fulfiled (4:14);*
> *This was to fulfil what was spoken by the prophet Isaiah (8:17); etc.*

This characteristic of Matthew's Gospel, his fondness for the Old Testament and for the fulfillment of its prophecies in Jesus, and his preference for the schematic ordering of his material have, quite naturally, elicited various theories about the shaping principle behind the Gospel as a whole. One of the most widespread and perduring of such theories is that Matthew arranged his Gospel into five books to correspond to the five books of Moses (the Pentateuch), which make up the Torah. Jesus is thus seen as the new Moses giving the new law on top of the mountain (of the Beatitudes in Mt. 5:1) and instructing his disciples on their mission (10:5), on the nature of the kingdom (13:11), and so on.

Yet, however attractive and convenient such a theory might be, it really does violence to the facts in Matthew's Gospel. It forces us to consider the first two chapters on the birth of Jesus and all the chapters on the Passion-Resurrection as no more than prologue and epilogue to the supposed five books. This, inevitably, underestimates the part these opening and closing chapters play in the Gospel. They are in fact very much a part and parcel of the whole development of Matthew's Gospel and not just useful additions.

But the most serious objection to the theory of five books consisting of five principal discourses (Mt. 5-7;10;13;18; and 24-25) is that it leaves no room for chapter 23. Now Matthew 23 is every bit as much of a solemn discourse as any in the supposed five books. Its importance for understanding Matthew's message, moreover, cannot be minimized.

Of course Matthew did have a guiding principle that dictated the shape of his Gospel and determined the selection and arrangement of the material that went into it. No one would want to deny Matthew's obvious concern with the fulfillment of the Old Testament prophecies in the person of Jesus. But there are other obvious concerns of the author in the Gospel besides that.

The attention Matthew gives to the "church" of Jesus Christ is all too well-known. One can cite as evidence Matthew's reworking of Mark's material in the famous confession of Peter at Caesarea Philippi. Not only does Matthew expand Peter's confession to:

"You are the Christ, the Son of the living God" (Mt. 16:16),

but he changes Jesus' command to secrecy in Mark 8:30 to a eulogy of Peter and combines it with a charge:

"Blessed are you, Simon Bar-Jona! For flesh and blood has not revealed this to you, but my Father who is in heaven.

> *And I tell you, you are Peter, and on this rock I will build*
> *my church, and the powers of death shall not prevail against*
> *it . . ." (Mt. 16:17-19).*

Another, perhaps less known, sample of Matthew's concern with the church is his remolding of Mark's account of the storm at sea (Mk. 4:35-41) into a miniature masterpiece of the beleaguered church at prayer (Mt. 8:23-27).

The Principle behind Matthew

The wide variety of concerns and the multiple characteristics that set it apart from the other Gospels have given rise, naturally enough, to many theories about the ruling principle behind the composition of Matthew's Gospel. The very multiplicity of theories is evidence of this Gospel's complexity. The insufficiency of each theory to explain the multiple facets of its author's genius have prompted scholars to try other approaches. Some have tried to get at its ruling idea by defining the situation which gave rise to it and the background against which it was written.

There are, for instance, several indications to favor its having been written for Jewish converts to Christianity. The reasons for this are not difficult to find. Not only Matthew's frequent appeal to the Old Testament but also his omitting to explain to his readers such Jewish customs and expressions as:

> *they make their phylacteries broad (Mt. 23:5);* or
> *whoever says Raca to his brother (Mt. 5:22,* where the RSV
> text explains: *"whoever insults his brother")*

seem to point in this direction. Jewish readers would not normally need any explanation of "phylacteries" or "Raca." Matthew, moreover, adapts Jesus' teaching on divorce to the Jewish views in the debate that was current at the time by inserting "except for unchastity" into the formal prohibition (Mt. 19:9 and 5:31-32).

Furthermore, Matthew is not content to stress the observance of the Law (Mt. 5:19); he has Jesus exhorting his hearers to "practice and observe" whatever the scribes and the Pharisees tell them (Mt. 23:2-3). Indeed, Matthew's longer version of the Our Father, to which we referred earlier, is perfectly comprehensible as an adaptation of the prayer to Jewish liturgical usage; even as his use of the "kingdom of heaven" for Mark's and Luke's "kingdom of God" is in deference to the Jewish respect for the sacred name of God.

But what is perhaps most cogent as an argument for setting Matthew's Gospel against a Jewish background is the puzzling "provincialism" of his Jesus:

> *"Go nowhere among the Gentiles, and enter no town of the Samaritans, but go rather to the lost sheep of the house of Israel" (Mt. 10:5-6);*
> *"I was sent only to the lost sheep of the house of Israel" (15:24).*

Yet, as one might suspect, even such arguments can be, and in fact are, countered by others that insist on Matthew's Gentile-Christian background. The "provincialism" of Jesus, for example, can easily be offset by the clearly universal dimensions of the concluding mission in the Gospel:

> *"Go therefore and make disciples of all nations . . ." (Mt. 28:19).*

There are of course other, subtler, ways in which Matthew opens wide the horizons of Jesus' ministry. In the explanation of the Parable of the Weeds (Mt. 13:36-43), which, like the parables of the pearl and the net, is found only in Matthew, Jesus says,

> *"the field is the world" (Mt. 13:38).*

In Jesus' dwelling in "Capernaum by the sea" Matthew sees the fulfillment of Isaiah's prophecy about

> *Galilee of the Gentiles—the people who sat in darkness have seen a great light—(Is. 9:1-2 in Mt. 4:12-16).*

It must be kept in mind, however, that Matthew's Gospel is not best seen as a factional document, for one group and against another. His views and aims are more global and his presentation of Jesus larger than could be readily fitted into any constricting framework. Therefore, one should take Matthew's Gospel as an integral whole, neither rigidly sectioning it off into a fixed number of books or discourses, nor pretending to present its Jesus simply in terms of favoring one group against another.

This is not to deny of course that there are clear and evident divisions in the Gospel: the birth and the infancy narratives in the first two chapters, which are so clearly an addition to the basic scheme we find in Mark; the various discourses of Jesus that form, together with the narrative that accompanies them, certain identifiable units; the great section on the Passion; and the final chapter on the Resurrection appearances, which is a further addition to the basic Markan framework.

It is also quite clear that Matthew is concerned with certain factions within the church. But it would be fairer to the evidence of the Gospel as a whole to regard them, not as factions of Jews against Gentiles, or of Jewish Christians against Gentile Christians, but rather as a dichotomy between those who believe in Jesus Christ and those who do not. Those that do believe, whether Jews or Gentiles, are the church. For, Matthew insists, the church is not a "new" Israel but the only true Israel. This is what he sets out to show throughout his Gospel; and in its light the factional conflicts will make better sense.

A Proposed Approach

It has been pointed out recently that one of the best ways to approach Matthew's Gospel and to grasp the shaping principle behind its structure and content is to see it as a threefold presentation of the person of Jesus: (1) Jesus' relation to the past; (2) Jesus' relation to the present: that of Jesus' contemporaries and that of Matthew's contemporaries; and (3) Jesus' relation to the future.

A. The first relation. It is quite easy to see how intent Matthew is to demonstrate Jesus' relation to Israel's past. Jesus' words and deeds are an accomplishment of the Old Testament prophecies. The miracles of healing fulfill "what was spoken by the prophet Isaiah, 'He took our infirmities and bore our diseases' " (Mt. 8:17; see Is. 53:4). Jesus spoke in parables

> to fulfil what was spoken by the prophet: "I will open my mouth in parables, I will utter what has been hidden since the foundation of the world" (Mt. 13:35; see Ps. 78:2).

But, more important still, every event in Jesus' life had been foretold or foreshadowed in the Old Testament. Matthew alone gives the details of Judas' betrayal and the price he got for it:

> *Then was fulfilled what had been spoken by the prophet Jeremiah, saying, "And they took the thirty pieces of silver, the price of him on whom a price had been set by some of the sons of Israel, and they gave them for the potter's field, as the Lord directed me" (Mt. 27:9-10; see Zech. 11:12-13; Jer. 32:6-15; 18:2-3).*

He is the only one to explain the entry of Jesus into Jerusalem on Palm Sunday with:

> *This took place to fulfil what was spoken by the prophet, saying, "Tell the daughter of Zion, Behold, your king is coming to you, humble, and mounted on an ass, and on a colt, the foal of an ass" (Mt. 21:4-5; see Is. 62:11; Zech. 9:9).*

His is the only Gospel that sees even in Jesus' going to dwell in Capernaum by the sea a fulfillment of "what was spoken by the prophet Isaiah" (Mt. 4:12-16; see Is. 9:1-2).

One might be inclined to think, after checking the above quotations against the Old Testament references, that Matthew's was not generally a very enlightened—according to our modern methods—approach to the Scriptures. He does not seem to quote word for word and is not very careful to give exact references. Yet Matthew goes farther still. The whole incident of the massacre of the infants by Herod seems to have had but one aim in view:

> *Then was fulfilled what was spoken by the prophet Jeremiah:*
> *"A voice was heard in Ramah, wailing and loud lamentation, Rachel weeping for her children; she refused to be consoled, because they were not more" "Mt. 2:17-18; see Jer. 31:15).*

Even the trip of the Holy Family to Egypt was:

> *to fulfil what the Lord had spoken by the prophet: "Out of Egypt have I called my son" (Mt. 2:15).*

But the nearest thing in any of the prophets seems to be Hosea 11:1

which is none too close. Of course, one can regard the whole Book of Exodus as a prophecy because it tells of Israel's deliverance from the bondage of Egypt (Ex. 4:22-23).

The thing to keep in mind in all this, however, is not how Matthew gets his Old Testament quotations and references but the use to which he puts them. It was remarked earlier, in speaking of the anonymity of the New Testament authors, that he must have been a genius of the first order whoever made that promise-fulfillment link between the Old Testament and Jesus. Matthew certainly carries out that fundamental theological insight with a thoroughness unrivalled by anything in the New Testament, with the sole exception perhaps of the Epistle to the Hebrews.

Matthew's thoroughness extended well beyond the fulfillment motif. Two of his favorite titles of Jesus are evocative of the whole range of messianic expectations in the Old Testament and the divine promises made to the house of David.

"Messianic expectations" is a catchall phrase for the hope that all those long-awaited promises of God to the Fathers and through the prophets will one day find their final and definitive fulfillment. The promised Messiah, the anointed one, came to embody the realization of those promises. Thus, when Matthew goes out of his way to remind his readers that this Jesus is "the Christ," which is the Greek translation of the Hebrew "Messiah," he is employing yet another promise-fulfillment device in the elaboration of his Gospel message.

Matthew, for instance, formulates the reason for the delegation of John the Baptist to Jesus thus:

> *Now when John heard in prison about the deeds of* the Christ *(Mt. 11:2).*

He alone among the Synoptics has Jesus say:

> *"You have one master, the Christ" (Mt. 23:10).*

He deliberately changed Mark 13:5, "I am he!" to

> *"I am the Christ" (Mt. 24:5).*

All these details, however minor they might seem, do in fact underline the messianic quality in what Matthew says about Jesus of Nazareth and his meaning.

Similarly, Matthew stresses Jesus' Davidic descent more than the other evangelists. He does this by structuring the genealogy of Jesus in three groups of fourteen (fourteen being the sum of the numerical value of the three letters which in Hebrew spell the name of David), and by tracing it to Joseph who is called the "son of David" (Mt. 1:20). He lays stress on Jesus' descent from the family of King David by his use of the title "Son of David":

> *"Can this be the Son of David?" (Mt. 12:23);*
> *"Have mercy on me, O Lord, Son of David" (15:22);*
> *"Hosanna to the Son of David!" (21:9).*

These passages in the Gospel will be all the more significant when, upon comparing them with Mark and Luke, we find out they are exclusively Matthean.

B. The second relation in the Gospel of Matthew, that of Jesus to the present, is a twofold relation. It regards Jesus' relationship to his own contemporaries; and, at the same time, it stresses his relationship to Matthew's own contemporaries.

In demonstrating Jesus' relationship to his contemporaries the Gospel insists on the great power that he exercised in his striking miracles, in his undeniable authority, and in the solemnity of his teaching. The effortless efficacy of the miracles is shown by such indications as:

> *And instantly the woman was made well (Mt. 9:22);*
> *And her daughter was healed instantly (15:28);*
> *and the boy was cured instantly (17:18);*
> *And the servant was healed at that very moment (8:13).*

The authority of Jesus is shown by the way Matthew describes him frequently as "ordering" and "commanding" the disciples (Mt. 8:18; 28:20), the crowds (14:19; 12:16) and the demons. The solemnity of his teaching is made evident by the formula "Amen I say to you," which in Matthew occurs thirty times on the lips of Jesus as against only thirteen times in Mark, six in Luke, and twenty-five in John.

On the other hand, Jesus' own contemporaries respond with the deference due a great personage. Matthew is fond of repeating phrases like "they came to him." He takes every opportunity to have people address Jesus as "Lord." It has been pointed out, for example, that, out of the nineteen times that Matthew has Jesus addressed by this great title, only two are actually found in his sources (i.e., in Mark or "Q").

Now, the title "Lord" is very especially a title that belongs to the Risen Jesus:

> *"Let all the house of Israel therefore know assuredly that God has made him both Lord and Christ, this Jesus whom you crucified" (Acts 2:36).*

When Matthew projects the title back into the public ministry of Jesus he presents the whole public ministry in the light of the subsequent Resurrection. That is, what the disciples came to believe about Jesus after he was risen from the dead came to be regarded as true of him even before his crucifixion. Indeed, Matthew is careful to insist that the title "Lord" was true of Jesus from the very moment of his conception "of the Holy Spirit" (Mt. 1:20).

As regards Jesus' relationship to Matthew's own contemporaries, the Christian community for whom Matthew was writing, we witness a parallel phenomenon at work. The crucified and risen Jesus now lives, just as he lived and taught in Palestine. The believing community responds to him not only by a profession of their faith confessing him to be Lord, Christ, Son of God. The response of their faith is not just a confession in words or by the use of honorific titles but an obedience to all that he commanded:

> *"teaching them to observe all that I have commanded you" (Mt. 28:20).*

Matthew's Gospel is really an illustration of obedience to this final command of Jesus. It is, to be sure, a proclamation of the good news; but it is also, and especially, an instruction, an exhortation, a "teaching to observe" all that Jesus commanded his disciples. Matthew must have taken this command of the Risen Lord as addressed to him personally. The Gospel he wrote was his own act of obedience to

> *"Go therefore and make disciples of all nations . . . teaching them to observe all that I have commanded you" (Mt. 28:19-20).*

But the task that Matthew fulfilled so admirably in writing his Gospel was not a solitary gesture. It had Matthew's own Christian community in view, its problems and dilemmas and quarrels. Unless we keep this fact in mind, the relevance of the instruction in the Gospel of Matthew will elude us.

Matthew insists, first of all, that the Christian community is a mixed one. That community, the church, is made up of "good and bad":

> *"And those servants went out into the streets and gathered all whom they found,* both bad and good*" (Mt. 22:10).*

That reminder, of course, remains as necessary for today's Christians as it ever was in Matthew's time. The Gospel is addressed to our present too. In this way it speaks to us after twenty centuries.

Matthew's conclusion of the Beatitudes, moreover, insists:

> *"Blessed are you when men revile you and persecute you and utter all kind of evil against you falsely on my account" (Mt. 5:11).*

It would be to misunderstand Matthew's intention in including these words were we to see in them a reference to evil from outside the community only. They make much more sense when we recall that, in the very next verse, those who "persecuted the prophets" (Mt. 5:12) were not from outside the community of Israel but from within it. Matthew knew in his time as well as we do today that the reviler, the persecutor, the abuser are not always outsiders.

This lends added poignancy to the prophecy in Matthew 24:10:

> *"And then many will fall away, and betray one another, and hate one another."*

He is the only evangelist to insert these words here (cf. Mk. 13:13 and Lk. 21:17). In Matthew 10:22 Jesus had already used similar words to describe the conditions of discipleship:

> *"Brother will deliver up brother to death . . . and you will be hated by all for my name's sake" (Mt. 10:21-22).*

The Christian church does not have to wait for the "last days" to see its members stumble, betray one another, and hate one another. It is certainly arguable that over the centuries Christians have suffered more at the hand of their fellow Christians than from those outside the faith. Matthew, evidently, knew whereof he spoke.

In very recent times attention has been drawn to yet another aspect of Matthew's concern for the present of his community of believers, the church. His is the only Gospel even to use the term "church." His concern for the role of Peter, the promises in Matthew 16:18-19, and the solemnity of the concluding mission (Mt. 28:18-20) have, understandably enough, made this Gospel a favorite of the church. But these qualities have also distracted from an equally genuine Matthean concern for that church. To understand this concern better we must recall some basic points.

The word of God, as we have had occasion to note before, is always addressed to a people, to a community of believers. Such community is of necessity hierarchical, howsoever unpalatable the term might seem to some today. The mere fact that there is a person chosen to be the bearer of God's word, to be a prophet or an apostle, sets up some hierarchical order. The community of believers in Christ was no exception to this rule. In this sense, the church is not and cannot be a democratic institution. It is, and always will be, a community that has leaders in its worship, teachers in its assemblies, and guides in its pilgrimage. It is a hierarchical church.

This hierarchical nature of the church is a thing that it has in common with most human societies. But there is a radical difference that sets it apart; and Matthew is the one New Testament author who describes this distinction best.

Around the second or third generation of Christians, at the time that Matthew's Gospel was composed, the Christian communities were beginning to reveal clearer patterns of their hierarchical structure. There were in its communities the leaders and the led, the teachers and the taught, the pastors and the flock. But, as in all human institutions, even the most "democratic", serious dangers threatened the life of the Christian community in the very exercise of that leadership.

Three different recent authors have called attention to indications of these dangers within the Gospel of Matthew. It would be best to describe the dangers separately even though they are very intimately linked.

Matthew, first of all, sees in the community of believers the real danger of a personality cult. It is precisely in that chapter 23, to which we referred above, that Matthew brings together sayings of

Jesus that make this concern quite explicit:

> *"But you are not to be called rabbi, for you have one teacher, and you are all brethren. And call no man your father on earth, for you have one Father, who is in heaven. Neither be called masters, for you have one master, the Christ" (Mt. 23:8-10).*

The triple format, the use of "the Christ," the Jewishness of the background in these words of Jesus are Matthean traits to which attention has already been drawn. We have grown used to the facile literal reading of the passage as though it were a protocol for Christian camaraderie or a manifesto against honorific titles in the Christian churches. But in fact these verses make sense both here and within the larger context of the Gospel only if they are seen as a prelude to the fundamental statement, repeated here from its original place in the source used by Matthew:

> *"He who is greatest among you shall be your servant; whoever exalts himself will be humbled, and whoever humbles himself will be exalted" (Mt. 23:11-12; and see Mt. 20:26-27 and Mk. 10:43-44).*

This is the genuine Christian antidote to the cult of personality. Greatness and primacy of place are, in the Christian community, titles only to humble service. What distinguishes the Christian community is not the abolition of all titles but the knowledge that leadership, under whatever name, is a service. In the Christian scheme such service is best rendered from a lowly position. It does not abolish greatness but redefines it:

> *"Whoever humbles himself like this child, he is the greatest in the kingdom of heaven" (Mt. 18:4).*

The verses in Matthew 23:8-10 are not then a prohibition of church hierarchy. They recognize the existence of a situation inherent in every society where there is need to exercise authority in any form; but they point out the two very real dangers within that situation: that of hypocritical authority and that of religious vanity.

This brings us to the second point that deserves notice here. The whole twenty-third chapter of Matthew has been entitled and construed as an invective against "the scribes and the Pharisees." It seems to form a climax of Matthew's anti-Jewish polemic throughout his Gospel. The whole Gospel has been seen as an example of that bitter antagonism, which attended the beginnings of Christianity, between the nascent church and the established synagogue.

The point that has often been overlooked in all this, however, is that Matthew's polemic is directed to a phenomenon within the Christian community itself. There is, to be sure, a marked antagonism to the Jewish leaders and to the synagogue in Matthew. But the far greater antagonism in the Gospel is directed not so much against the Jews or the scribes as against the hypocrites within the Christian community itself. Matthew, as one author has put it, was "more concerned with the hypocrisy of church leaders than with those of synagogue leaders."

Matthew knew that two temptations would face church leaders: to become either false prophets or hypocrites. It is to these perennial dangers of ecclesiastical leadership that he addresses himself in chapter 7, which forms part of the Sermon on the Mount:

> *"Beware of false prophets, who come to you in sheep's clothing but inwardly are ravenous wolves" (Mt. 7:15),*

and also in chapter 23, which is an attack not so much on "rabbinism" as on "clericalism":

> *"Woe to you, scribes and Pharisees, hypocrites!" (Mt. 23:13,23,25,27,29).*

It would be all too easy to read these two chapters as though they had been addressed only to those "scribes and Pharisees" outside the church's community. A close attention to the audience addressed in these discourses and especially to the words that Matthew puts on the lips of Jesus should make us realize that the Gospel's concern was the instruction of the Christian community on genuine concerns and problems in its midst.

Finally, the third point to be noted is the very major role assigned Peter in the Gospel of Matthew. There is no doubting Peter's place of preeminence among the twelve apostles: he is the first called (Mt. 4:18) and the first named in the list of apostles (10:2). Matthew's is the only Gospel to add to the incident of the walking on the water in

Mark 6:45-52 the story of Peter's misadventure (Mt. 14:28-31); and, to the confession at Caesarea Philippi in Mark 8:27-30, the "Blessed are you, Simon Bar-Jona!" (Mt. 16:17-19). His is the only Gospel to report the incident of the temple tax (Mt. 17:24-27), in which Peter plays an important role; and the only one to have Peter occasioning the "seventy times seven" response from Jesus (Mt. 18:21-22).

Peter's role in the Gospel of Matthew, however, is not without ambiguity. He is the prototype of the church leader. Yet, for all his preeminence—or perhaps because of it—he is particularly prone to stumble and fall: after the confession at Caesarea Philippi, during the walking on the water, and in the Passion. He is, in other words, not only subject to grievous temptations but also very apt to fall ignominiously.

It would be all too easy to say that, after the Resurrection, Peter left his failures and foibles behind, that thenceforth he would never falter. But that would be wholly to misconstrue not just the nature of Matthew's Gospel but also its aim. Matthew is, as we have had occasion to note, projecting back into the public ministry of Jesus the reality of the Risen Lord. He is not talking of what had been, but of what was in his own time.

In other words, as a contemporary author has put it, Matthew is our witness that we do not have to wait for the triumph of the Emperor Constantine in order to begin to see the church being subjected to the temptations of power. The establishment of Christianity as the state religion after the victory of Constantine brought immense dangers and temptations to the church. But we do not have to wait to the fourth century to see this. The church of Matthew's time, like the church in every age, already had its share of false teachers and false prophets. They were neither outsiders nor limited to the rank and file in the Christian community.

Peter's black-and-white portrait in Matthew will remain an enigma forever unless we remember this fact. It is a portrait not to confound but to comfort the weak and to make the mighty within the church reflect. No dogmatic definition could ever reverse this to allow us to act and think as though Matthew's portrait of Peter was meant to confirm the mighty in their power and inspire dread in the hearts of the lowly.

C. The third relation, that of Jesus to the future, in the Gospel of

Matthew would require a whole chapter to itself and inevitably raise questions that take us far afield. For this reason, only two points need be made here:

(1) It is precisely in those contexts which discuss the future that Matthew speaks, in highly figurative language, of the punishment of the wicked. No other book of the New Testament uses the word "hell" so frequently; and no other Gospel is so graphic in its description of it. The real tragedy—and it is nothing short of this—is the persistent tendency of Christians to take such passages in the Gospel independently of the work of Matthew as a whole, without any regard for the literary forms of the utterances or for their history, and with a mindless insistence on changing what are figures of speech into actual realities.

If the dangers of the monolithic, literal interpretation of the New Testament seemed overstressed in the earlier chapters, then the interpretation of Matthew's use of the future punishment of the wicked can serve as one justifying example. This interpretation has, over the centuries, not only persistently refused to abide by any of the norms of literary or historical criticism, but it has also steadfastly clung to the "very words of Jesus," turning the good news of Matthew into the dread tyranny of fear. They have turned the kingdom of heaven into a reign of terror.

(2) The good news in Matthew is seen not only in God's great fidelity to his past promises of salvation, nor only in the reign of the Risen Lord over the present community of believers, but also and especially in the vision of the future. This future, both of the individual Christian and of the Christian community, is seen by Matthew in function of the demands of the present. The life we lead here and the call that the present moment makes upon each one of us are what we will be judged by in the future. The judge is the Christ. His norm for judgment is:

"I was hungry and you gave me food,
I was thirsty and you gave me drink,
I was a stranger and you welcomed me,
I was naked and you clothed me,
I was sick and you visited me,
I was in prison and you came to me"
(Mt. 25:35-36).

Here, as also in the good news of Mark, the criterion of service is the only acceptable response to the proclamation of the Gospel.

Perhaps that great genius whom we call Matthew has left us, like some Renaissance artist, a self-portrait in the very act of composing his Gospel:

> *"Therefore every scribe who has been trained for the kingdom of heaven is like a householder who brings out of his treasure what is new and what is old" (Mt. 13:52).*

Might not the writing of the Gospel according to Matthew have been the response in service of that one scribe so well "trained for the kingdom of heaven"? There are after all more ways of feeding the hungry and comforting the prisoners than are dreamt of in our sociology.

6   Luke's Narrative

Here at last, one might say with relief, is a Gospel written in the best historical tradition of the ancients. For what could be more specific and historically accurate than:

> *In the fifteenth year of the reign of Tiberius Caesar, Pontius Pilate being governor of Judea, and Herod being tetrarch of Galilee, and his brother Philip tetrarch of the region of Ituraea and Trachonitis, and Lysanias tetrarch of Abilene, in the high-priesthood of Annas and Caiaphas, the word of God came to John the son of Zechariah in the wilderness"* (Lk. 3:1-2)?

No other evangelist goes to such lengths to date so precisely the beginning of John the Baptist's public ministry and, consequently, to fix the date of the start of Jesus' public ministry. And it all checks.

The author of the third Gospel was evidently at pains not only to give the exact historical bearings of the events but also to explain carefully, in a proper introduction to his work, what it is he set out to do and why:

> *Inasmuch as many have undertaken to compile a narrative of the things which have been accomplished among us, just as they were delivered to us by those who from the beginning were eyewitnesses and ministers of the word, it seemed good to me also, having followed all things closely for some time past, to write an orderly account for you, most excellent Theophilus, that you may know the truth concerning the things of which you have been informed (Lk. 1:1-4).*

The Greek of this superbly constructed sentence, as of the rest of the Gospel, is elegant and far superior to Mark's. The whole opening

106

sentence is a marvel of balance and symmetry, the work of an author not unacquainted with the lofty traditions of eloquence in antiquity. The credentials he offers are impeccable; the statement of his purpose, unexceptionable.

The author of this introduction is very clearly a second generation Christian. By the time he came to write, "many" had already preceded him. He was quite conscious of not undertaking something wholly new; others before him had undertaken to compile a narrative "of the things which have been accomplished among us." He was also aware of being an heir of a tradition that had been delivered "from the beginning." Of the reliability of this tradition he had no doubt. It came from "eyewitnesses and ministers of the word."

What the author himself intended to do was to set down an "orderly account." But his aim was more than to "compile a narrative" in an orderly fashion. It was more than just to hand on what had been delivered to him by tradition. He wanted to write in such a way as to let the "most excellent Theophilus" know the true meaning of the things about which he had been, to translate the word literally from the Greek, "catechized."

The nuances of this final phrase in the introduction are not easy to capture. It is instructive to see how other modern English translations render it. The *New English Bible* translates it, "so as to give you authentic knowledge about the matters of which you have been informed"; the *Good News Bible* reads, "so that you will know the full truth about everything which you have been taught"; the *Jerusalem Bible* has, "so that your Excellency may learn how well founded the teaching is that you have received;" and the *New American Bible*, "so that Your Excellency may see how reliable the instruction was that you received." But however you choose to read it, it certainly says that its author is going to be more than a Xerox machine or a tape recorder.

Theophilus is to us an unknown, almost as unknown as this Greek-speaking author who produced the longest work we have in our New Testament. The Gospel of Luke is in fact only the first part of a two-volume work, whose second volume is the Acts of the Apostles (see Acts 1:1-2). The fact that parts one and two do not follow one another in our New Testament is incidental. The Gospel of Luke and the Acts of the Apostles belong together and form one unified work.

The identity of the author of this two-volume work has captured the Christian imagination from the very beginning. Tantalizing clues in the writings of Saint Paul as well as an old tradition going back to the early centuries have made it difficult to imagine Luke as any other than "the beloved physician" that Colossians 4:14 speaks of. Scholars have gone so far as to isolate the "medical vocabulary" of the author to bolster up the argument in favor of the identification. But the whole romance of Luke the beloved physician has to be subjected to critical scrutiny.

The meager available evidence is inconclusive. The medical vocabulary used by Luke can be shown in equal abundance in contemporary authors who we know for a fact were not physicians. Moreover, to identify the author of Luke-Acts with Paul's "fellow worker" mentioned in his Epistle to Philemon:

> *Epaphras, my fellow prisoner in Christ Jesus, sends greetings to you, and so do Mark, Aristarchus, Demas, and Luke, my fellow workers (Philem. 23-24),*

seems rather unlikely. If the author was really the fellow worker of Paul mentioned in his letter to Philemon then he could not have listened too carefully to what Paul had to say. The divergences in their ways of thinking about and understanding of the meaning of Jesus Christ are such that, many are convinced, the author of Luke-Acts and the fellow worker of Paul could not have been one and the same person. Others, of course, would argue that such divergences are indicative of independence of judgment and no more.

But, whoever the author of Luke-Acts was—and we shall simply call him by his traditional name, as we usually do in speaking of the other evangelists, he left us a monument of his genius that is impressive in every way. Not only is the work among the most accomplished in the New Testament from a literary point of view; but, with its breadth of vision, one of the most imposing statements of the relation of the church to its Lord and to the world.

The purpose of the whole undertaking is stated by the author to be:

> *that you may know the truth concerning the things of which you have been informed (Lk. 1:4).*

This stated purpose embraces both parts of the work. For, at the start of the second book, Luke makes explicit reference to the work accomplished in the first:

> *In the first book, O Theophilus, I have dealt with all that Jesus began to do and teach, until the day when he was taken up, after he had given commandment through the Holy Spirit to the apostles whom he had chosen (Acts 1:1-2).*

Evidently then, the work and teaching of Jesus was only a beginning. It was a beginning that was meant to be carried on in response to his command "through the Holy Spirit" to the apostles he himself had chosen. The second book is a record of how that command was carried out after Jesus was "taken up." The author is very aware of a difference between the two periods in time, but he is equally aware of the continuity between them, between the work of Jesus and that of his apostles.

This vision of the Christian event is unique to Luke. His Gospel is not merely a narrative of all that Jesus said and did. It is an account of only the first part of an event that continues right into the life of the church. There is for Luke a profound unity between the two parts of the one event that brings "good news of great joy" to all the earth (Lk. 2:10).

It is therefore not surprising to find that Luke has maintained a remarkable parallelism between the two parts of his work. This happens to be only one important device he employed for underlining the continuity between the two and the identity of the event narrated in both. Thus, both books open in Jerusalem: Zechariah in the temple of Jerusalem (Lk. 1:8-9), and the apostles waiting in Jerusalem (Acts 1:4).

The ministry of Jesus opens with:

> *the Holy Spirit descended upon him in bodily form, as a dove (Lk. 3:22)*

at the baptism. The missionary activity of the apostles similarly begins with:

> *There appeared to them tongues as of fire, distributed and resting on each of them. And they were all filled with the Holy Spirit (Acts 2:3-4).*

at Pentecost.

Jesus on his cross prays:

> *"Father, forgive them; for they know not what they do" (Lk. 23:34).*

Stephen, the first Christian martyr, cries out with a loud voice:

> *"Lord, do not hold this sin against them" (Acts 7:60).*

This parallelism extends to smaller details as well. But the important thing to keep in mind here is that all these observations should make us careful how we understand that "truth concerning the things of which you have been informed." This should be extended to embrace both the Gospel and the Acts. The fundamental insight of the author into the meaning of the saving event of Christ Jesus governs both volumes. The good news proclaimed by the words and deeds of Jesus goes on being proclaimed by the words and deeds of those whom he has chosen.

We need to be reminded of this because it is so very easy to leap to the conclusion that the "truth concerning the things of which you have been informed" has to do, first and foremost, with the historical veracity of the account. It is so tempting to see Luke as *the* historian among the evangelists.

But this would be to miss the true genius of Luke. It would be to assess his accomplishment by the standards of the ancient Greek and Roman historians, when in fact it should be gauged against the only really comparable achievements of Mark, Matthew and John. Such an attitude to the Gospel of Luke would, moreover, presume that the "things of which you have been informed," the matters about which Christians have been catechized, are historical data as such.

This is the perennial temptation of so many Christians: the notion that we believe because there is solid historical evidence for our beliefs. It is all too easy to forget that faith in Jesus Christ, in Luke's time as now, rests on much more than the historical verifiability of the words and deeds of Jesus of Nazareth. It rests on much more than the historical accuracy of what we can know about him.

Any careful student of the Gospel of Luke will be struck by elements that, on any reading, cannot be regarded as models of "historical" research and accuracy. Here, as in Matthew, comparison with Mark and with the parallels in Matthew will urge a different view. Having given, for instance, the exact historical background of the start of the ministry of John the Baptist with such detail (Lk. 3:1-2), why does Luke leave the geographical particulars of the baptism so vague? Mark and Matthew clearly say John's ministry was "in Judea." Why is Luke content to leave it at "the region about the Jordan" (Lk. 3:3), omitting any mention of Judea whatsoever? If the reason for this is "historical accuracy," then he is obviously correcting Mark and Matthew but without offering any reason or explanation. If, however, the reason for this variation introduced by Luke at this point is other than historical, then it should fit a pattern of variations in the rest of the Lukan account. There should be, in other words, an explanation for this difference in Luke that is other than historical.

Thus, it is not accuracy nor a sense of fidelity to the facts as they actually happened that prompted Luke to have John the Baptist locked up in prison (Lk. 3:20) before the baptism of Jesus (Lk. 3:21). Indeed, Luke omits the mention of John from the baptism altogether, simply stating:

and when Jesus also had been baptized (Lk. 3:21).

These, admittedly minor, variations are in the account of an event of major importance in the life of Jesus. To claim "historical accuracy" for their author does not seem to make much sense. But to seek an explanation for them elsewhere would invest them with worth and significance. Evidently, the truth "concerning these things" lies a bit beyond the accurate reporting of who, when and where. The "accuracy" of the catechetical instruction that Luke seeks to safeguard and insure is not historical but theological.

Why then all these historically detailed underpinnings of the Lukan narrative? Why all this accumulation of accurate historical information in Luke 1:5; 2:1-2; 3:1-2? The reason is simply this: For Luke, Christ and his continuing work are firmly grounded in history. Jesus' life was not marginal to the great Roman Empire; it was an integral part of it. The life of his church is also not tangential to the great events of history but, like it or not, a determinant part of it. Luke, in other words, can help us see clearly why in our Creed even today we still say: "He was crucified *under Pontius Pilate.*" The good news is part and parcel of everyday history.

Salvation History

Many authors over the centuries have called attention to Luke's concern with "salvation history." This can be misleading. It can suggest that there is some history entirely distinct from and independent of "secular history." But, for Luke, "salvation history" takes part within and in the ordinary course of events of world history. It is not something parallel to it, nor something taking place in some supernal realm above the earth. This is why Luke is so careful to specify the historical circumstances of "the things which have been accomplished *among us*" (Lk. 1:1).

There is in fact just one history; and the life of Jesus of Nazareth—as also the life of his church—is an inseparable part of it. This is why even those scholars who are thought to be most extreme in their views about Jesus and the New Testament would consider any doubt about whether Jesus of Nazareth really existed as utterly absurd and not even worth refuting. Luke is always there to remind all of us that "the things of which you have been informed" took place—and are taking place—right here in our own history. The merciful salvation that was promised for ages (Lk. 1:69, 72) has not been realized somewhere out of time and out of this world. It is not some celestial drama of which a report has reached us in the act of divine revelation. It is something that has taken place "among us" (Lk. 1:1):

> *in the fifteenth year of the reign of Tiberius Caesar, Pontius Pilate being governor of Judea . . . (Lk. 3:1-2).*

But this is not all. It is not the least of Redaction Criticism's merits to have called our attention to Luke's very special concern with time and with the stages of salvation history. Luke does see the history of salvation unfolding in stages. He sees the time of Jesus within the whole scheme as central to all that went before and all that was to come after it.

It is therefore for a very good reason that Luke formulates the words of Jesus about John the Baptist differently from Matthew. Luke's citation of Jesus' words reads:

> *"The law and the prophets were until John; since then the good news of the kingdom of God is preached, and every one enters it violently" (Lk. 16:16).*

This is quite different from Matthew's:

> *"From the days of John the Baptist until now the kingdom of heaven has suffered violence, and men of violence take it*

> *by force. For all the prophets and the law prophesied until John; and if you are willing to accept it, he is Elijah who is to come" (Mt. 11:12-13).*

Luke thus sees John the Baptist as the close of a chapter in the history of salvation. That chapter has to terminate before the new one begins. This, by the way, is a clue to why Luke thought it necessary to remove John the Baptist from the scene and lock him up in prison before the baptism of Jesus and the start of his public ministry.

Luke also sees the time of Jesus as a specific, defined period. That period, which is covered by the Gospel part of the Lukan work, is the "midpoint of time." It is no less neatly set off from what follows it in the Acts of the Apostles than is the John the Baptist narrative from the account of Jesus' ministry in the Gospel. Luke found it necessary to recall to his readers of Acts that the first part, the Gospel, dealt:

> *with all that Jesus began to do and teach, until the day when he was* taken up *(Acts 1:2).*

In other words, Luke found it necessary to remove Jesus physically, so to speak, from the scene at the end of that period. The Gospel ends with:

> *he parted from them (Lk. 24:51);*

and Acts repeats and expands this into the whole tableau of the Ascension:

> *he was lifted up, and a cloud took him out of their sight (Acts 1:9).*

At the end of the Gospel, the apostles, obedient to the command of the Lord to

> *"stay in the city, until you are clothed with power from on high" (Lk. 24:49),*

returned to Jerusalem

> *with great joy, and were continually in the temple blessing God (Lk 24:53).*

At the beginning of Acts, just prior to the descent of the Spirit at Pentecost, we are reminded again that they

with one accord devoted themselves to prayer (Acts 1:14).

But what is interesting to note is that Luke, right at this point (Acts 1:13), gives us again the list of the apostles which he had already given in Luke 6:14-16, minus of course the "Judas Iscariot, who became a traitor."

What Luke does here is to stress the continuity between this stage of the church in Acts and that which preceded and prepared for it in the Gospel. It is far more important to emphasize this continuity between the stages of salvation history in Luke rather than the lines of demarcation that set off one stage from the next.

The second part of the Lukan work, the Acts of the Apostles, remains in fact an open-end work. For having charted the progress of the nascent church and the missionary labors of its great apostles, the author leaves off his account with the Apostle Paul

preaching the kingdom of God and teaching about the Lord Jesus Christ quite openly and unhindered (Acts 28:31).

If we recall that Luke wrote these words some twenty-five or thirty years after this event took place, after Paul's arrival in the city of Rome and long after his death, then we can understand better how they are meant to be a prelude to what is yet to come and not a conclusion to what has already been.

Luke thus sees his own time as yet another chapter of the Acts, else he would have rung the curtain down with the martyrdom of the Great Apostle and so set up yet another parallel with the Gospel. The fact that he does not is an invitation to his readers to see their own history as part of the ongoing event of salvation.

Perhaps Luke understood better than many of the theologians who followed him down the centuries that the perpetual newness of Christianity consists in the regenerative power latent in every event of its history. We read Luke-Acts not in order to amass information about the past but to understand how that past is at work in our own present and, above all, to see how even now the past is "good news of great joy" for our future.

This is why, more recently, New Testament scholars have pointed out that, in Luke's work, the stages of the history of salvation are not as sharply marked as some have hitherto made them seem. There is, in other words, a greater consciousness of the continuity between the prophets and Christ, and between Christ and the church. The picture that Luke presents is not static. It shows the progressive movement from the prophets to Christ, and from Christ to the apostles down to our own day. The whole movement is, moreover, under the moving power of one and the same Holy Spirit.

The Holy Spirit

The Holy Spirit is the true and principal reason for the continuity in the work of Luke. It underlies the parallelism between Jesus' baptism and the church's Pentecost. It moves and guides the whole course of history from its inception to its consummation.

It is the same Holy Spirit that "inspired" the old Simeon (Lk. 2:27), that "filled" Jesus and "led" him for forty days "in the wilderness" (Lk. 4:1). It is the same Holy Spirit that the Risen Lord promises to send on the apostles (Lk. 24:49) that "fills" them and "gives them utterance" on the day of Pentecost (Acts 2:4).

Luke's vision of the history of salvation is very much a vision of the activity of the Holy Spirit through the ages. It is this same Holy Spirit who has been and continues to be the agent of divine revelation through the prophets, through Christ, and through his church (Acts 28:23-28).

The Christology

We have thus far seen three of the principal characteristics that mark the work of Luke: (1) Luke's view of the history of salvation and its stages; (2) his linking of the history of the church to the history of Jesus by writing the two-part work of Luke-Acts and not just a Gospel according to Luke; and (3) his delineation of the action of the Spirit both in the life of Jesus and in the life of the church.

These three concerns make sense only in the light of what Luke thinks of Christ, in other words, in the light of his Christology. Each of the Gospels presents its own answer to "What think you of the Christ?" Any answer given to this question is, in the last analysis, a Christology. Thus, the Christology of each evangelist necessarily marks and shapes his entire undertaking. His own response to

"What think you of the Christ?" will not only determine the evangelist's choice of details but his interpretation of them. Indeed, we have already examined how that Christology shaped Mark's view of discipleship and Matthew's reading of the Old Testament. Now we must try to see how Christology also shaped the work of Luke.

Perhaps the easiest approach to this would be to see first what Luke has done with the material he had to work with. We note, for instance, that he is careful to remove any offensive features from Mark's account of Jesus. Mark 1:34 says Jesus "healed many"; Luke 4:40 makes it "every one of them." In Mark 3:5 Jesus "looked around at them with anger, grieved at their hardness of heart." This, in Luke 14:10, becomes simply, "And he looked around on them all." Even when, in Mark 10:21, Jesus "looking upon [the rich young man] loved him," Luke has a laconic "he said to him" (Lk. 18:22). Of course, such a remark in Mark 3:20 as "He is beside himself" is omitted altogether by Luke. He also substitutes for Jesus' dying words in Mark 15:34:

> "*My God, my God, why hast thou forsaken me?*"

the prayer:

> "*Father, into thy hands I commit my spirit!*" (*Lk 23:46*).

The Poor

Yet, paradoxically enough, Luke's Jesus is also the great lover of all the despised and dispossessed of this world: the poor, the sinners, the Samaritans, and women. Luke's is very much a gospel of the downtrodden and the poor. Not only is the "good news of great joy" announced first to the traditionally humble and poor, the

> *shepherds out in the field, keeping watch over their flock by night (Lk. 2:8-10);*

but the principal actors in the whole drama are themselves poor.

There is in the Lukan account of Jesus' birth no "wise men from the East" who open their treasures and offer gifts of "gold, frankincense and myrrh" (Mt. 2:1, 11). The offering that the parents of the child make in the temple is just "a pair of turtledoves, or two young pigeons" (Lk. 2:24). The "law of Moses" that Luke refers to in this passage is clear enough:

> And if she cannot afford a lamb, *then she shall have two turtledoves or two young pigeons (Lev. 12:8).*

Indeed, the whole act of God's redemption in Christ Jesus is summed up in the canticle that Luke includes in his account of the birth of Jesus:

> *"he has put down the mighty from their thrones, and exalted those of low degrees; he has filled the hungry with good things; and the rich he has sent empty away" (Lk. 1:52-53).*

But Luke is not content to leave Jesus' love for the poor as a theory or a theme in the Gospel. He makes it explicit in the teaching of Jesus. The first Beatitude, as we have already seen, became simply:

> *"Blessed are you* poor; *for yours is the kingdom of God" (Lk. 6:20; cf. Mt. 5:3).*

To this Beatitude Luke adds the parallel:

> *"But woe to you that* are rich; *for you have received your consolation" (Lk. 6:24).*

This saying of Jesus has nothing to correspond with it in the Gospel of Matthew. Jesus' advice to the rich young man in Mark 10:21:

> *"go, sell what you have"*

becomes in Luke:

> *"Sell* all *that you have" (Lk. 18:22).*

Luke alone of the evangelists includes such parables as the Rich Fool (Lk. 12:13-21):

> *"A man's life does not consist in the abundance of his possessions" (Lk. 12:15);*

the Unjust Steward (Lk. 16:1-13), and the Rich man and Lazarus, "the poor man . . . full of sores" (Lk. 16:19-31).

But Luke is not content to leave the question of poverty as an example or an exhortation. In his second volume he gives little vignettes of how the church was to live out this poverty and this love for the poor in its daily life:

> *And all who believed were together and had all things in common; and they sold their possessions and goods and distributed them to all, as they had need (Acts 2:44-45).*
> *Now the company of those who believed were of one heart and soul, and no one said that any of the things which he possessed was his own, but they had everything in common (Acts 5:32).*

These are idyllic pictures, and their author knows them to be such. They are not a description of a golden age now past. Anyone tempted to misread such passages in Acts for what they were never meant to be, to see in them factual descriptions of a Christian utopia or the basis for a Christian communism would do well to read, not just passages in Paul like Galatians 2:11 or 1 Corinthians 11:17-22, but Lukan narratives in the book of Acts itself.

Those who believed, even the most illustrious among them, were not always of "one heart and soul":

> *But when Cephas came to Antioch I opposed him to his face, because he stood condemned (Gal. 2:11).*

They did not give everything they had to the poor:

> *When you meet together, it is not the Lord's supper that you eat. For in eating, each one goes ahead with his own meal, and one is hungry and another is drunk (1 Cor. 11:20-21).*

They did not even share equitably among the needy:

> *the Hellenists murmured against the Hebrews because their widows were neglected in the daily distribution (Acts 6:1).*

The Sinners
In Luke the love of Jesus for sinners is not just the "good news" proclaimed by the angels at his birth:

"For to you is born this day in the city of David a Savior,
who is Christ the Lord" (Lk. 2:11).

It is a love that Luke shows to be operative and effective throughout
the life of Jesus. Luke alone tells us the story of the sinner who wet
the feet of Jesus "with her tears, and wiped them with the hair of her
head" (Lk. 7:36-50). Twice he repeats that

> *tax collectors and sinners were all drawing to him (Lk. 15:1-
> 2 and 5:29-30).*

It is he who says that the sheep in the parable is "lost" (Lk. 15:4) and
not, as Matthew 18:12 has it, "gone astray." And it is Luke who
gives us the charming story of Zaccheus, "chief tax collector, and
rich . . . and small of stature" (Lk. 19:1-10).

Of course, only Luke records that jewel of New Testament literature, the Parable of the Prodigal Son (Lk. 15:11-32):

> *"But while he was yet at a distance, his father saw him and
> had compassion, and ran and embraced him and kissed
> him" (Lk. 15:20).*

Luke too is the only one of the evangelists to insert into the account
of the crucifixion the story of the two criminals and Jesus' promise:

> *"Truly, I say to you, today you will be with me in Paradise"*
> *(Lk. 23:43).*

The Samaritans

Along with Jesus' love and care for sinners and the poor, Luke
tells of his love for the Samaritans, the despised minority of the day.
Had the evangelist done no more than given us the portrait of the
Good Samaritan (Lk. 10:29-37), he would have more than adequately conveyed the reality of Jesus' love for them. But to this
parable Luke adds the account of the healing of the ten lepers (Lk.
17:11-19), of whom only one "turned back . . . giving thanks."
"Now," adds Luke, "he was a Samaritan."

Luke of course omits Jesus' stern injunction to the apostles in
Matthew 10:5:

> *"Go nowhere among the Gentiles, and enter no town of the
> Samaritans."*

Even when he recounts a Samaritan village's rejection of Jesus (Lk. 9:51-56) he brings in one of the dominating motifs of his Gospel as an explanation to mitigate it:

> *And he sent messengers ahead of him, who went and entered a village of the Samaritans, to make ready for him; but the people would not receive him,* because his face was set toward Jerusalem *(Lk. 9:52-53).*

The proclamation of the message to Samaria in Acts (1:8; 8:5,14) would, of course, more than offset even that momentary rebuff.

The Women

Luke's above all is the Gospel of women. He alone of the Synoptics recounts the incidents of Martha and Mary (Lk. 10:38-42), of the healing of the woman "who had a spirit of infirmity" (13:10-17), and of the raising of the widow's son at Nain (7:11-17). Only Luke tells us:

> *And the twelve were with him,* and also some women *who had been healed of evil spirits and infirmities (Lk. 8:1-2).*

He even lists the names of some of these women and adds:

> *and many others, who provided for [Jesus] out of their means (Lk. 8:3; cf. Acts 16:15).*

This, however, is not the whole extent of Luke's concern. No one can read the first two chapters of his Gospel, the Infancy Narrative as they are called, without being struck by the role that Mary plays. Into her mouth Luke puts one of the New Testament's most beautiful canticles, a perfect compendium of God's act of salvation in Christ Jesus (Lk. 1:46-55). Mary's attitude throughout the events narrated sums up all those traits in her that, according to the canticle she utters, find favor in the eyes of God: the fear of the Lord, humility, lowliness and poverty.

> *"He has shown strength with his arm, he has scattered the proud in the imagination of their hearts, he has put down the mighty from their thrones, and exalted those of low degree;*

he has filled the hungry with good things, and the rich he has sent empty away" (Lk. 1:51-53).

We can perhaps best illustrate Luke's attitude by seeing the use he makes of one incident in Mark's Gospel. The way that Mark 3:31-35 narrates the incident of Jesus' mother and brothers asking for him and Jesus' response about who his true mother and brothers are gives some inescapable hint of a polemic against the relatives of Jesus. Perhaps the community of Mark was experiencing some problems with some relatives of Jesus. Perhaps the evangelist found it necessary to remind his own community that, in a similar conflict of interests, Jesus' response was stern and clear:

"Who are my mother and my brothers?" And looking around on those who sat about him, *he said, "Here are my mother and my brothers! Whoever does the will of God is my brother, and sister, and mother" (Mk. 3:33-35).*

We simply do not know the circumstances that prompted Mark to narrate this incident, which is anything but complimentary to Jesus' mother and brothers.

Now, it is instructive to observe how Luke radically alters the whole account. He recounts the coming of Jesus' mother and brothers, and tells of their desire to see him. But the whole passage in Mark becomes simply this in Luke:

But he said to them, "My mother and my brothers are those who hear the word of God and do it" (Lk. 8:21).

There is no looking about him, no pointing to them that sat about him, as though he deliberately meant to exclude his blood relatives at the door. There is just a simple statement, which is universal in its application, and intended not as a polemic against anything so much as an exhortation to something: to hearing the word of God and doing it.

This deliberate change by Luke will not be lost on his attentive readers. This mother of Jesus is she who, at the very beginning of Luke's Gospel, says:

"Behold, I am the handmaid of the Lord; let it be to me according to your word" *(Lk. 1:38).*

Luke goes on to define Mary's true claim to greatness in the incident of the woman in the crowd who cried out:

> *"Blessed is the womb that bore you, and the breasts that you sucked!"*

To which Jesus responds:

> *"Blessed rather are those who hear the word of God and keep it!" (Lk. 11:27-28).*

Luke makes sure too that, at the beginning of Acts, we find again the mother of Jesus and the women:

> *All these with one accord devoted themselves to prayer* together with the women and Mary the mother of Jesus, *and with his brothers (Acts 1:14).*

Summary and Conclusion

Luke's method in his two-volume work had a larger aim than the adaptation and the expansion of Mark's Gospel or the extension of the account into the history of the community in Acts. His care to show the links of Jesus with secular history and to present the whole history of Jesus as an integral part of world history also had a wider purpose. To this aim and to that purpose we must now turn both to summarize and to conclude.

The imposing work of Luke is a reminder to Christians that the history of Jesus is a new beginning, the beginning of the history of the church. Neither history is fully intelligible without the other. The Acts of the Apostles is not an incidental appendage to the Gospel, but an integral part of an as yet unconcluded whole.

Luke, of course, is interested in the antecedents of this history which he narrates. It is new in relation to what is old. But Luke's approach to the Old Testament is quite different from Matthew's. In Luke the relation of the Old Testament to the New is not only that of promise to fulfillment. It is a relation that finds its intelligibility in God's continuing love for man throughout history. In this sense we can speak of salvation history.

This love of God is directed particularly to those who are despised by men and accounted by them as lost: the poor, the lowly, the dispossessed and the disinherited of this earth. To all these, Luke reminds us, the love of God comes as a present redemption in the person of Jesus. The coming of Jesus to the poor, the sinners, the Samaritans and women is the glad tidings of great joy. Luke's work constantly reiterates the theme of this joy in salvation:

> *"And you will have joy and gladness, and many will rejoice at his birth" (Lk. 1:14);*
> *"for behold, I bring you good news of a great joy which will come to all the people" (2:10);*
> *"Rejoice in that day, and leap for joy" (6:23);*
> *"And the disciples were filled with joy and with the Holy Spirit" (Acts 13:52).*

Moreover, the Jesus of Luke's Gospel teaches and instructs his disciples for their future mission in the community. Luke inserts into the Markan framework, between the end of chapter 9 and the beginning of chapter 10 in Mark, a lengthy section (Lk. 9:51—18:14), which has but a few real parallels in either Mark or Matthew. In this section Luke gathers traditions about Jesus that are particularly suited to show the preparation of the disciples for their future work: the ready mercy of the Good Samaritan (Lk. 10:29-37); the need and value of prayer (10:38—11:13); the need for constant watchfulness and for the avoidance of entanglement in earthly things (12:22-48); the need for humility (14:7-14); the need for genuine caring illustrated by the father of the Prodigal Son (15:11-32) and by the concern of the good shepherd for those who are "lost" (15:1-10) and not merely gone astray.

The whole work of Jesus is thus seen by the evangelist as a preparation of the disciples for their post-Easter task. Jesus' own stay on earth is seen as a steady ascension to Jerusalem:

> *When the days drew near for him to be received up, he set his face to go to Jerusalem (Lk. 9:51).*

This verse happens to be the geographical midpoint of the Gospel of Luke. It explains his care to keep Jerusalem and Judea out of the picture till the appointed time (recall his description of the Baptist's ministry and his avoidance of specifying Judea as the place of the baptism). Jerusalem is, of course, the place where Jesus is crucified and only in it (not in Galilee as in Matthew, Mark and John 21) does the Risen Jesus appear.

It is from Jerusalem that Jesus ascends to heaven (Acts 1:9-10), bringing to a close that very special time in history when he walked among men. His last charge to the disciples before he leaves them is both an assurance and a mission:

> *"But you shall receive power when the Holy Spirit has come upon you; and you shall be my witnesses in Jerusalem and in all Judea and Samaria and to the end of the earth" (Acts 1:8).*

The Acts of the Apostles then takes the narrative from Jerusalem itself to "the end of the earth."

Thus, in a way, Luke recounts the whole history of Jesus backwards from the history of the present church (Acts 10:36-43). His work is a superb illustration of the reading back into the life of Jesus the situation of the believing community. All genuinely living tradition does this, of course. But Luke goes it one better. He explains the real reason behind this: as in the life and ministry of Jesus, so too in the life and ministry of his church, it is one and the same power that is acting, filling, moving and directing:

> *"The Holy Spirit will come upon you, and the power of the Most High will overshadow you" (Luke 1:35);*
> *And they were all filled with the Holy Spirit (Acts 2:4).*

7   The Word of John

To move from the Synoptics to John is not to move to a new world but to be granted a new vision of the same one. In those ancient symbols of the four evangelists (see Ezek. 10:14) the eagle is the one chosen to represent the fourth evangelist. Not only does an eagle dwell in lofty places and soar to great heights; but, it is popularly believed, his is the keenest of visions and his eyes alone can gaze steadily at the sun. The choice of that symbol for John the Evangelist was unerring.

As long ago as the second century, Saint Clement of Alexandria recognized John's as the "spiritual gospel." Not only does it tell so well the relation between Jesus and the Spirit, but its whole content and meaning require more than the ordinary comprehension needed for literal truth. It is a Gospel that calls for the best that interpreters of any age can bring to any text. But, over and above that, it requires—as one of its earliest commentators remarked in the third century—that whoever presumes to interpret it must have, like its author, "lain close to the Master's breast" (see Jn. 21:20).

So advanced is the theology of the Fourth Gospel that its author has, from the earliest centuries, merited the name of "the theologian." In more recent times, this same highly developed theology has convinced many great scholars that John's Gospel could not have been written much earlier than the latter half of the second century, sometime after A.D. 150. Such a view, of course, went counter to the solidly maintained tradition that the "beloved disciple" of whom the Gospel speaks is the apostle John who wrote the Fourth Gospel.

The Gospel itself offered evidence to support what the tradition firmly held:

> *He who saw it has borne witness—his testimony is true, and he knows that he tells the truth (Jn. 19:35);*
> *This is the disciple who is bearing witness to these things, and who has written these things; and we know that his testimony is true (21:24).*

Yet, against both one and the other, scholars persisted in dating the Gospel at a time when the "beloved disciple" will have had to be at least 140 years old.

In this instance, however, historical evidence was to confound the propounded theories of the scholars. Two archaeological discoveries in this century compelled them to revise their dating of John radically. The discovery of the Qumran manuscripts in Palestine in 1947 revealed a world of ideas not only native to the land of Jesus' ministry but contemporary with it. Scholars realized that you really did not have to go outside Palestine nor wait a hundred years after the death of Jesus in order to explain the elaborate and complex ideas we meet in the Gospel of John.

The second discovery, made some years before Qumran, was in Egypt. The results of this archaeological great fortune did not achieve the attention and the notoriety they deserve till rather recently. The manuscripts found in Qumran were Jewish and of the first century or earlier; those found in Egypt were from the early centuries of Christianity.

Among the manuscripts uncovered in Egypt were some of the oldest manuscripts we have of our New Testament. Till their discovery, the earliest New Testament manuscripts we possessed went back only to the fourth century. Some of the manuscripts found in Egypt date back to as early as the second century. The earliest among them, curiously enough, is a tiny fragment containing verses from John 17: 31-34.

Scholars date this tiny fragment to between A.D. 130 and 150, that is, to just about fifty years after the date that tradition usually assigned to the Fourth Gospel. This date of the manuscript fragment is in itself a most remarkable fact. To appreciate its full import you have to keep in mind the time it took to copy a whole Gospel by hand, to have it spread from one Christian community to another, to have it travel the very considerable—for those times—distance that separated modern day Turkey, the traditional place where John is thought to have been written, from Egypt, where the fragment was actually found. When you take all these factors into consideration, fifty years is almost too short a time for the Gospel of John to reach Egypt.

To any skeptic disposed to dismiss three or four verses of one chapter from the Gospel of John as insufficient evidence, the sands of Egypt had more evidence still. There was unearthed a copy of the entire Gospel of John (chapters 1 to 14 have a few bits missing; chapters 15-21 are only in fragments). Scholars date this manuscript to about A.D. 200.

All this should explain why today New Testament scholars are unanimously agreed that the Gospel of John was written when tradition maintains it was written, that is, sometime in the last decade of the first century, between the years 90 and 100. This is all the more striking when we reflect on what John's Gospel actually says about Jesus, about the Christology of the first century. Within that Christology the titles conferred on Jesus in the Fourth Gospel are among the very highest we possess anywhere in the New Testament. From this point of view alone the Gospel of John merits not just the accolades tradition conferred upon it but also the loving attention the church has lavished on it in its liturgy and theology, its preaching and teaching, its art and its mysticism.

The Author of the Fourth Gospel

If the early dating of the Fourth Gospel resolved one major conflict between scholarship and tradition, it has not had the same effect in the debate on the identity of its author. This debate goes on unabated even now. But, though a conclusion is nowhere in sight, it is rather difficult to dismiss out of hand the Christian Palestinian roots of much that we find in the Gospel of John. It is almost as difficult to dismiss the link that this Palestinian tradition has with the "beloved disciple."

Whether this "beloved disciple" is to be identified with John the son of Zebedee, however, or with anyone else is very difficult—if not impossible—to decide. Some of the most bizarre identifications have been, and continue to be, proposed. But it is the part of prudence to admit yet again our ignorance of the real identity of the author of the Fourth Gospel. It is, in other words, not easy to demonstrate convincingly that "he who saw it" in John 19:35 and "the disciple who is bearing witness to these things, and who has written these things" in John 21:24 are to be identified with one another and with John the son of Zebedee as the "beloved disciple."

Comparison with the Synoptics

What is more important for our understanding of the Gospel of John than the identity of its author is, of course, its content. For, it is truly unique among the four Gospels. It is perhaps the only genuine rival of Mark for the accolade of originality.

If the author of the Fourth Gospel knew the Gospel of Mark, as seems quite likely, then he used its content with a freshness of outlook and a breadth of vision unmatched by either Matthew or Luke. Whether John knew these other two Gospels as well is still hotly debated. But, whatever the extent of his acquaintance with one or all of the Synoptics, John evidently had access to traditions about Jesus that were quite different from those available to them.

The very striking difference in John's chronological and geographical framework of Jesus' ministry would in itself be sufficient indication of this. If you follow Mark's dating and sequence of events, then Jesus' public ministry must have lasted barely a year. At the start of the ministry we have the indication that the grain is ripening (Mk. 2:23); and at its close there is mention of "the Passover and the feast of Unleavened Bread" (Mk. 14:1): so from late spring to the following spring. This scheme is of course also followed by Matthew and Luke.

John's Gospel, on the other hand, mentions at least three Passover feasts during the public ministry of Jesus: after the marriage at Cana (Jn. 2:13); at the multiplication of the loaves (Jn. 6:4); and the final Passover of the Passion (Jn. 11:55). So, by this reckoning, Jesus' public ministry lasted at least two years.

Moreover, the geography of that public ministry also differs in John. In the Synoptics Jesus' ministry took place in Galilee until his journey to Jerusalem and his crucifixion. In John, however, Jesus goes from Galilee to Jerusalem thrice: during the Passover feast after the marriage at Cana (Jn. 2:13); after healing the official's son (Jn. 5:1); and at the feast of Tabernacles (Jn. 7:10). On this last trip Jesus stays about six months in Jerusalem, from the feast of Tabernacles to the Passover of his Passion (Jn. 18:28).

A far more important, though perhaps not as evident at first reading, difference is the tradition about Jesus' deeds and words. The Synoptics, as we have already seen, take the individual events and disparate sayings of Jesus and put them together. John, however, uses his material quite differently. He has accounts of various events (e.g., the marriage at Cana in Jn. 2:1-10, the cleansing of the temple in 2:13-21, etc.). Like the Synoptics, John also has a long, continuous account of the Passion. But, in the Gospel of John, the events seem almost subsidiary to the discourses that follow them. They are there, it seems, only as a prelude to the discourses that follow them. The cure of the man who had been ill for "thirty-eight years," for example, is followed by a long discourse by Jesus in chapter 5.

In the Synoptics the different sayings of Jesus are grouped together into a series (like the parables in Matthew 13) or into groups of sayings (like the Sermon on the Mount in Matthew). But in John the discourses of Jesus are quite different. They take a theme and elaborate it by a dialogue (as, for example, the theme of a new birth in the dialogue with Nicodemus in John 3); or in a debate (such as that in John 8), or in a monologue like that on the Good Shepherd in John 10.

But what is even more remarkable than any of these differences is the language that Jesus speaks in the Fourth Gospel. It is not just the difference between the individual aphorisms in the Synoptics and the sustained discourses in John; nor is it the prevalence of parables in the former and their scarcity in the latter; nor just the distinctive vocabulary that Jesus uses in John's Gospel. The difference in language is such as to evoke two worlds of thought, two distinct spheres of ideas. This difference is so remarkable it has prompted scholars to date the Gospel of John late in the second century, as we have seen already.

The language of Jesus in John's Gospel is strongly marked by contrasting pairs of ideas: light and darkness, from above and from below, truth and falsehood. Throughout the Gospel Jesus speaks in "I am" statements:

> *I am*
> *the bread of life (Jn. 6:35, 41, 48);*
> *the light of the world (8:12; 9:5);*
> *the door of the sheep (10:7, 9);*
> *the good shepherd (10:11, 14);*
> *the Son of God (10:36);*
> *the resurrection and the life (11:25);*
> *the way, and the truth, and the life (14:6);*
> *the true vine (15:1).*

Thus, the whole saving work of Christ is given a different expression in John. Themes like the bread of life in John 6, the new birth in John 3, or the living water in John 4, describe the work of salvation in Jesus Christ quite differently from the Synoptics. Just compare, for instance, the climactic statement in Mark:

> *"For the Son of man also came not to be served but to serve, and to give his life as a ransom for many" (Mk. 10:45)*

with the statement in John:

> *"I am the good shepherd. The good shepherd lays down his life for the sheep" (Jn. 10:11).*

Indeed, so great is the difference in language that when, for once, Jesus says in the Synoptics:

> *"All things have been delivered to me by my Father; and no one knows the Son except the Father, and no one knows the Father except the Son and any one to whom the Son chooses to reveal him" (Mt. 11:27; Lk. 10:22),*

commentators have been quick to point out the very "Johannine" manner of his speech (compare Jn. 3:35; 5:20; 13:3). The passage has even been called a "Johannine thunderclap in the Synoptic skies."

The Johannine Polemics

The fundamental question to be asked of all this accumulation of observable data is: What is the author of the Fourth Gospel trying to do? There are, as indicated in previous chapters, conflicts of opinion on this precise point in each of the first three Gospels. It is only to be expected that, in the case of the Fourth Gospel, the opinions are more numerous and more divided still.

The reader of John's Gospel will be struck by several bitter polemics against various groups of people. Consequently, there have been scholars who insisted that one of these polemics can best explain the aim and purpose of the evangelist. In other words, they propose either one given polemic or a combination of them as adequate explanation of the motive that prompted the author to write the Gospel.

Thus, for example, because of the sharp—and unfavorable—contrast between Jesus and John the Baptist in the very opening pages of the Gospel as well as elsewhere, authors have suggested that a polemic against the followers of John the Baptist is the motive behind the writing of the Fourth Gospel. John the Baptist "was *not* the light but came to bear witness to the light" (Jn. 1:8). Jesus is the "*true* light" (1:9). He ranks before John (1:15). His testimony is greater than that of John (5:36). John is not the Christ (1:20, 3:28). He worked no miracles (10:41). The Fourth Gospel insists that, unlike John the Baptist:

> *Jesus himself did not baptize, but only his disciples (Jn. 4:2; and see 3:22-24).*

But the most decisive argument against the Baptist are the words he himself utters:

> *"He must increase, but I must decrease" (Jn. 3:30).*

If, as seems likely, there was a sect that followed John the Baptist rather than Jesus at the time of the writing of the Fourth Gospel, then these indications will have served as arguments in a polemic against that particular sect. Nevertheless, though they are careful to assign John the Baptist his proper place in relation to Jesus, the passages quoted from the Gospel of John cannot but strike an impartial reader as really more laudatory of the Baptist than condemnatory of his followers. Moreover, when the Gospel is taken in its entirety, the polemic against the followers of the Baptist can at most be regarded as only one motive among many in the author's design. It is certainly not the ruling force behind the whole Fourth Gospel.

Another, far sharper, polemic is more in evidence throughout the Gospel of John. It is the polemic against "the Jews." That there is the bitterest opposition to "the Jews" in this Gospel cannot be denied: "the Jews persecuted Jesus" (Jn. 5:16); they sought "to kill him" (5:18; 7:1); they have never heard the voice of the Father and do not have his word abiding in them (5:37-38); Moses himself accuses them (5:45); they do not even believe the writings of Moses (5:47); none of them "keeps the law" of Moses (7:19).

The history of the misreading, misinterpretation and misapplication of such and similar passages in John's Gospel is well known. It reflects no credit on Christians and less on their hearing of the word of the Father. If there is one single example where the tragedy of the monolithic interpretation of the Scriptures is seen at its clearest, then the Gospel of John must be it. All that was said in the opening chapters of this book can find reason and illustration here: the fact that any interpretation bears the mark of the prejudice and the background of the interpreter; the ease with which personal preferences are elevated to expressions of the divine will; the pernicious—and the word is not too harsh—insistence on "the very words of Jesus" in the New Testament; and the consequent evasion of the fact that the authors of the New Testament are human, limited, conditioned human beings, bearing the marks of their time and their background even when they speak the word of God to us.

In order to appreciate at its true harshness this polemic against the Jews in the Gospel of John we must recall a few simple facts of history. Whether or not they received him, Jesus did come "to his own people" (Jn. 1:11). He lived and died a Jew among Jews. The author of the Fourth Gospel knew that, however persistent later Christians might have been in ignoring it. John also knew that the disciples of Jesus were Jews:

> "Behold, an Israelite indeed, in whom is no guile!" (Jn. 1:47).

He knew too that many Jews "believed in him" (Jn. 8:31; 11:45; 12:11). No interpreter of the Gospel can afford to forget these simple facts.

Why then the polemic against the Jews in the Fourth Gospel? The answer to this must be sought in the background against which the Fourth Gospel was written. The first Christians were largely Jewish Christians, Jews who, as John 12:11 puts it, had gone away and believed in Jesus. The first Christians were, consequently, little more than a small Jewish sect among so many other Jewish sects of the period. They were so regarded by those around them, whether Jews or Romans.

After the destruction of Jerusalem by the Romans in A.D. 70, a real rift began between the Jews and the Christians. That rift took various forms and had many motives, the religious motive having been only one of them. It is only after that fateful date that our Gospels began to be written; and the Gospel of John came toward the end of the first century, when the positions of the Jews and the Christians had hardened considerably.

It is only with this background in mind that the polemics of the Fourth Gospel against the Jews can make any sense at all. This can be well illustrated in the incident of the blind man in John 9. The fear of the parents to respond to the questions put to them by the Jewish authorities is explained thus by John:

> For the Jews had already agreed that if any one should confess him to be the Christ, he was to be put out of the synagogue *(Jn. 9:22; cf. 12:42)*.

Such a statement would make no sense whatsoever either in the lifetime of Jesus himself or in that of the first generation of Christians. If read into the lifetime of Jesus, it would make utter nonsense of most of Paul's letters and all of the Acts of the Apostles, where we are told that after the Ascension the believers in Jesus were

> *day by day, attending the temple together (Acts 2:46).*

The expulsion, at a much later date, of Jewish converts to Christianity from the synagogue must surely have been one of the sorrows that weighed heavily on the heart of John's community. It underlay much of the polemic against the Jews in his Gospel. Nevertheless, for all its presence throughout, it is not in and of itself an adequate explanation of the ruling idea behind the Gospel of John. Any reader can see that other concerns also had a claim on the author's attention.

A third polemic in the Gospel of John is one against Christian heretics of the first century. Their heresy is called Gnosticism. The tendency to explain the Fourth Gospel as a polemic against this heresy is very modern and quite in vogue; but it has illustrious and ancient ancestry going as far back as Saint Irenaeus in the second century.

This approach to John's Gospel sees in its insistence on the fact that the Word

> *was in the beginning with God; all things were made through him (Jn. 1:2-3)*

a firm stand against the Gnostics who held that matter, being of its nature evil, had to be created not by God but by some lesser deity. John's Prologue, this approach maintains, is one indication of his combatting that heresy.

Moreover, some of the peculiarities of the Johannine style, to which reference was made at the beginning of this chapter, are also seen in the Gnostic writings that are known to us. This is adduced as further evidence that John was using their own language to refute them. He describes Jesus, for instance, as the true revealer; and, in doing so, he is insisting on the falsity of the Gnostic revealer. John uses "knowledge"—which in Greek is *gnosis,* from which we get Gnostic and Gnosticism—almost as an equivalent of saving faith. Faith in Christ is the true knowledge, he insists; and this is seen as yet another aspect of his polemic against the Gnostics.

But the most telling blow against the heretics in John's Gospel is not so much against one specific heresy as against a quality which marks a great many heresies. It is a heresy called Docetism. It maintains that Jesus only *appeared* to be man, whereas in reality he was God. In other words, underlying the attitude of Docetism is a mistrust of and a low esteem for the human, the material, for what in biblical language is called "flesh and blood." Against this position the Gospel of John, for all its exaltation of Christ, takes an unequivocal stand:

> *And the Word became flesh and dwelt among us (Jn. 1:14).*

This is a statement that no true Gnostic would accept, and any form of Docetism would find impossible to explain.

*"Amen, amen, I say to you, unless you eat the flesh of the
Son of man and drink his blood, you have no life in you; he
who eats my flesh and drinks my blood has eternal life" (Jn.
6:53-54).*

Such words put on the lips of Jesus would put beyond all cavil any
question about the true humanity of the Son. Should this still leave
room for doubt, the author of the Fourth Gospel calls the testimony
of an eyewitness to corroborate the flesh-and-blood reality of Jesus:

*But one of the soldiers pierced his side with a spear, and at
once there came out blood and water. He who saw it has
borne witness—his testimony is true, and he knows that he
tells the truth—that you also may believe (Jn. 19:34-35).*

No stand in the Gospel of John is so clearly and unshakably firm
as this stand against Docetism in all its forms. The First Epistle of
John is, if anything, even more adamant:

*That which was from the beginning, which we have heard,
which we have seen with our eyes, which we have looked
upon and touched with our hands . . . (1 Jn. 1:1).*

One unfailing test of the true Christian in this same Epistle is
precisely to confess that:

Jesus Christ has come in the flesh *(1 Jn. 4:2).*

If this negative aspect of John's Gospel is belabored, it is for a
reason. Such Docetism, such mistrust of the human, such opposition
to all flesh-and-blood, has wider ramifications and more far-reaching
implications than the question of Christ's true humanity. It is at the
heart of the problem of reading the Bible as the word of God.

Every position that tends to maximize the "of God" and to
minimize the "of man" in a formula like "The Bible is the word of
God in the word of man" is ultimately Docetic. Any attitude that
seeks to dispense the reader of the Bible from the demands of literary
and historical criticism, pretending that God somehow dispenses
with such means in the communication of his message, is but a thinly
disguised form of Docetism. Such an attitude imagines it a religious

virtue to exalt the perfect and the infallible in the divine, and to deny the very imperfect and very often quite fallible human element in its communication.

Against such an attitude, the Gospel of John's

And the word became flesh (Jn. 1:14)

can serve as a warning. It warns against a misunderstanding not just of the Incarnation but also of the means that God uses to make its mystery known to us. It cautions against the dangers of misinterpreting not only what the good news says but also how the good news is communicated.

In the final analysis, however, it would be grossly unfair to misunderstand the Gospel of John were we to read it only as a polemic against the John the Baptist sectarians, the Jewish opponents of Christianity, or the Gnostic and Docetic aberrations of Christian believers. These negative elements are there, to be sure; but they are subservient to a larger, more positive purpose. This purpose is expressed clearly and forthrightly by the author:

> *Now Jesus did many other signs in the presence of the disciples, which are not written in this book; but these are written* that you may believe *that Jesus is the Christ, the Son of God, and that believing* you may have life *in his name (Jn. 20:30-31).*

The Gospel of John, written for Christian believers, has this supreme aim in view: to believe that Jesus is the Christ, the Son of God; and, as John sees things, to have this faith in Christ is to have life. The aim of the Gospel, therefore, is not twofold but single. All other aims—and there is no denying their presence and their multiplicity in the Gospel—cohere and make sense in this one aim: "that you may believe."

> *For God so loved the world that he gave his only Son, that whoever believes in him should not perish but have eternal life (Jn. 3:16).*

Every testimony adduced by the evangelist is to that single purpose.

From the witness of John the Baptist:

> *that all might believe through him (Jn. 1:7);*

to the eyewitness at the crucifixion:

> *that you also may believe (Jn. 19:35).*

The Plan of the Gospel

To obtain a better grasp on how this aim of the evangelist is realized we should look more closely at the way he structured his Gospel. We have already remarked the chronological and geographical modifications that John introduces into the material familiar to us in the Synoptics. His modifications, however, went well beyond these.

The Jesus of John, for instance, does not perform miracles but "works signs." He does not "speak in parables" but uses "comparisons." He eats the Last Supper *before* the Passover (Jn. 13:1); whereas in the Synoptics Jesus ate a Passover meal with his disciples on the night before he died (Mk. 14:12). So in John, Jesus even dies on a different day. For, he was condemned to die at noon ("about the sixth hour") on "the day of Preparation of the Passover" (Jn. 19:14) just about the time that the priests would have begun slaughtering the lambs for the feast.

Such differences, though surprising, are quite comprehensible within John's vision of his task and his plan for its execution. The attempts to reconcile everything in the Fourth Gospel with the Synoptics are not always satisfactory nor very convincing. But, of course, this is the fault neither of John nor of the Synoptists. It is the fault of the misconceived notion that a harmony between the Gospels must be found because we imagine them to be historical biographies of Jesus of Nazareth, telling the unerring truth in our own way. It results from misunderstanding the very real and irreconcilable differences between the four Gospels because we expect them to furnish us with information that was not within their ken.

If John's data are irreconcilable with the Synoptics then the explanation is to be sought, not in their geography or in their chronology, but in the individual theological vision of each of their authors. To get some idea of the vision that inspired the Fourth Gospel we should examine how it is structured, recalling that what an author chooses and his arrangement of the material he chooses can tell us much about the ruling idea behind his work as a whole.

The Gospel of John clearly has both a Prologue (Jn. 1:1-18) and an Epilogue (Jn. 21). The Prologue is, in a true sense, a summary introduction to all the basic themes of the Gospel: God, life, light, faith, witness, the world, new birth, children of God, flesh, truth, glory, knowledge. The Epilogue, on the other hand, whatever the difficulties it presents to the interpreter, is in a genuine sense a resumption and summary of what was in the main body of the Gospel: the reference to Cana, the reinstating and commission of Simon Peter, the fate of "the disciple whom Jesus loved," and several other details all draw together and round off the Gospel material.

Between these two points, between the "beginning" of the Word with God in John 1:1 and the abiding task of the "Follow me!" that the Word commands in John 21:22, there are two major sections. There is the "Book of Signs" (Jn. 1:19-12:50) and there is the "Book of Glory" (Jn. 13:1-20:31).

The first part of the Gospel is usually called the Book of Signs because it comprises the very symbolic seven "signs":

> *the wedding at Cana (Jn. 2:1-11);*
> *the healing of the official's son (4:46-54);*
> *the paralytic of Bethesda (5:1-15);*
> *the multiplication of the loaves (6:1-15);*
> *the walking on the water (6:16-21);*
> *the healing of the blind man (Jn. 9); and*
> *the raising of Lazarus (Jn. 11).*

On the other hand, the Book of Glory is so called because it recounts the glorification of the Son when:

> *his hour had come to depart out of this world to the Father (Jn. 13:1).*

That is the hour when the Father glorifies the Son (17:1). It includes, in John's view of things, the whole Passion, the crucifixion itself, and the resurrection and exaltation of the Son. Thus, John's view even of the crucifixion of Jesus is necessarily different from the other evangelists'.

So the movement of return to the Father in John's Gospel is one uninterrupted sweep from the beginning of chapter 13 to the close of chapter 20. Within this vast sweep the very crucifixion of Jesus is seen by the evangelist as a being "lifted up from the earth" (Jn. 12:32), an exaltation. On that very cross the whole work of Christ is accomplished. Jesus' last word on the cross is:

"It is finished" (Jn. 19:30);

and with this last word he

gave up his spirit (19:30).

Thus, the crucifixion of Jesus is seen by John as the consummation of all his work, his own exaltation to and glorification by the Father, and his giving of "the spirit" to all who believe in him.

Throughout the Gospel, the whole purpose of the Son's coming to "dwell among us" (Jn. 1:14) is precisely the gift of life to anyone who believes in him:

"I came that they may have life, and have it abundantly"
(Jn. 10:10).

His teaching is a gift of life:

"The words that I have spoken to you are spirit and life"
(6:63).

And, in an incident resembling the confession at Caesarea Philippi in the Synoptics, Simon Peter says it all very well:

"Lord, to whom shall we go? You have the words of eternal
life; and we have believed, and have come to know, that you
are the Holy One of God" (6:68-69).

It is therefore not surprising to see the whole Book of Signs variously orchestrating this same theme:

the beginning of new life (Jn. 2:1-4:42);
the life-giving Word (4:46-5:47);
the bread of life (Jn. 6);

the light of life (Jn. 7-8);
the judgment by the light (9:1-10:21);
the victory of life over death (11:1-53); and
life through death (12:1-36).

Moreover, as John sees things, the whole of Israel's past searching of the Scriptures had but one purpose:

"You search the scriptures, because you think that in them you have eternal life" (Jn. 5:39).

Like the Synoptists before him, John knew that those Scriptures pointed to only one thing:

"It is they that bear witness to me" (Jn. 5:39).

Little did the author of the Fourth Gospel suspect that one day Christians would turn to his own composition in their search of the Scriptures in order that they too might come to know

"the way, and the truth, and the life" (Jn. 14:6).

In turning to the Gospel of John they have never been disappointed.

It is this Gospel above all others that insists on the personal nature of the Christian search of the Scriptures. John's Gospel is the one that insists most on the personal nature of the encounter with Jesus; the one that stresses the personal element (see Nicodemus in John 3; the woman of Samaria in John 4; and Lazarus in John 11). Consequently, the various individuals in the Fourth Gospel tend to become paradigmatic for the believer. That is to say, they become to the reader of the Gospel examples of the faith in and the response to the person of Jesus: the mother of Jesus, the blind man, the beloved disciple.

The whole of John's Gospel is, moreover, a re-interpretation of the life of Jesus in the light of the Scriptures. Its author tells us as much:

His disciples did not understand this at first; but when Jesus was glorified, then they remembered that this had been written of him *and had been done to him (Jn. 12:16).*

He thus puts all the events of Jesus' life within the perspective of anyone who hears the message of the crucifixion and glorification of Christ proclaimed in any age.

So the Gospel of John is, above all, a truly creative re-interpretation of the life of Jesus in the light of the community's faith, beset as that community was by threats from without and dissensions within. John knows that Jesus is, in a very real sense, away:

> *"I did not say these things to you from the beginning, because I was with you. But now I am going to him who sent me" (Jn. 16:4-5).*

The situation of the disciples is not very different from ours. Jesus is not "with us" in that sense any more. This is the whole meaning of:

> *"Blessed are those who have not seen and yet believe" (Jn. 20:29).*

Whatever the rhetoric of religious sentiment many employ, and no matter how vividly the imagination is brought into play, the Jesus in whom we believe can no longer be heard, or looked upon, or seen with our eyes, or touched with our hands (cf. 1 Jn. 1:1).

But the community of believers is not left "desolate" (Jn. 14:18) by this real absence of Jesus from them:

> *"These things I have spoken to you while I am still with you. But the Counselor, the Holy Spirit, whom the Father will send in my name, he will teach you all things, and bring to your remembrance all that I have said to you" (Jn. 14:25-26).*

This "remembrance," this process of recall, of being instructed and taught, is ultimately the reason behind our Gospels. This is why believers continue to search the Scriptures:

> *"It is they that bear witness to me" (Jn. 5:39).*

The Gift of Life

The motive force behind this search of the Scriptures, this need of "remembrance," is something that Christians have in common with all truly religious people of whatever faith. We search the Scriptures because we think that in them we have life, eternal life (Jn. 5:39). Our unending search for the word of God is really a search for life, a search for a way out of the impasse of death. This has nothing to do with our courage or cowardice to face death. It has nothing to do with our pitiable attempts to avoid it or delay its coming. It simply recognizes, almost with the integration of instinct, the reality of death in human life.

The search of the Scriptures, moreover, is not for the passing pleasure of the intellectual quest, nor for the amassing of learning. It is a search in quest of life, in quest of redemption from the predicament of death. Our searching the Scriptures is a quest of life. This is why we say that the word of God is living.

The answer that the Gospel of John gives to this quest is very simply this: In Christ Jesus we have been given the gift of eternal life. That, and that alone, is the solution to our dilemma.

> *"And this is eternal life, that they may know thee the only true God, and Jesus Christ whom thou hast sent" (Jn. 17:3).*

Of course this "knowledge" is not just an abstract intellectual exercise. It is rather the personal knowledge that begets love of the one known. It is the knowledge that begets a life lived, not a dogma elaborated in lofty accents.

This is why, in the Fourth Gospel in particular, the life which that knowledge of "the only true God, and Jesus Christ whom thou hast sent" begets is a life of love. This love, in turn, is not in the realm of fuzzy sentiment, nor measured by the warmth of inner feelings. In John's Gospel there can be no evading its imperative:

> *"If you love me, you will keep my commandments" (Jn. 14:15).*

The "commandments" are, of course, reducible to one only commandment:

> *"This is my commandment that you love one another as I have loved you" (15:12).*

There is no need to ask how this is to be carried out. The whole account of the Passion is a description of the meaning of love, of how he himself loved us:

> *Having loved his own who were in the world, he loved them to the end (13:1).*

*"Greater love has no man than this, that a man lay down his
life for his friends" (15:13).*

With this we have, in a way, come full cycle to the Gospel of
Mark. The discipleship that found its definition in service and
suffering there, finds its redefinition in terms of love and suffering
here. And, lest any reader misunderstand the "greater love has no
man" as an exclusive reference to the grand gesture of martyrdom,
the author of John adds:

*"You are my friends if you do what I command you"
(15:14).*
"This I command you, to love one another" (15:17).

Conclusion

The argument against what was called a "fundamentalist" approach to the New Testament is not based so much on any basic error in that position as on the ultimate inadequacy of its conclusions. God, of course, could reveal directly to an individual, inspiring him and preserving him from error. But for that revealed message to be of any use to me here and now, I need to postulate a similar inspiration and preservation from error for every copyist, textual critic, translator and commentator of the Bible.

This too is not inherently impossible. An omnipotent God can surely do this. But the argument of this book is precisely that the God in whom Christians believe, judging by the evidence we have to hand, does not do this. This God, it is argued, leaves human beings to be what they are, does not multiply spectacular interventions in order to make his truth prevail, and is not above becoming man and being in all things human in order to communicate the mystery of his love to us.

It is argued, moreover, that a fundamentalist approach, whether espoused by an individual or upheld by an institution, will ultimately out. Those who maintain that the Bible is literally and infallibly the word of God make for themselves the claim, willy nilly, of divine inspiration in some form or other. An institution like the Catholic Church claims infallibility. An individual Christian would claim the gifts of the Spirit. In either instance the claim can be traced to the way divine revelation is understood, to the way in which the Bible is said to be the word of God. Ultimately, of course, it can be traced to the way that institution or that individual understands how God saves us in Jesus Christ.

But to pursue this line of argument would be the object of another book not this one. What this book has tried to do is examine the facts as they are available to us, arguing from what we have today, how it came to be what it is, and the means we have to interpret what it says. The examination was, by prior option, limited specifically to the words of Jesus and to the Gospels which report them.

Keeping in mind that the present exposition assumes as its own one of two possible approaches—both of which it acknowledges to be legitimate, its argument against the rejected approach is mostly by way of illustration from the Gospels. For, in addition to the lack of thoroughness in its arguments and the failure to carry them to their necessary conclusions, the fundamentalist position inevitably runs the risk of the tryanny of its presuppositions. This risk is most evident in its use of the Gospels.

If I believe that what I have in these words of Jesus in the Gospel of Matthew is the very word of God, then it is only natural that I should wish to impose that word on myself—it is hoped—and to subject others to it. There is nothing wrong with this unless you happen to believe that reading the word of God, or of anybody else, requires interpretation; and interpretation is never 100% objective. It is precisely the element of subjectivity in interpretation, particularly in the interpretation of the word of God, that is suspect. We are all so ready to make of our own preferences the will of God.

In other words, a good deal—if not all—of what is claimed to be the word of God is in reality the word of man. It is not just the word of some prophet or apostle, but of some individual or institution here and now who is every bit as conditioned by background, limited in understanding, and circumscribed by prejudice as the inspired authors. If my faith embraces the original prophets and apostles as bearers of God's word to me, need I extend that faith to every interpretation of that word? If my faith extends to my church's tradition because the community of believers to whom I belong sees the truth of that tradition and believes it to be holy, must I extend that faith to every Christian individual or community that makes a claim here and now?

A Christian or a community of Christians can and does believe that the word uttered by a certain individual is the word of God. But this is a free option not a reasoned conclusion. Indeed, Christians can and do believe that the Gospel of John is the word of God even while they have a good idea of how the Gospel came about, the strange circumstances that necessitated its composition, and the multiplicity of interpretations to which it is open.

With Saint Paul, Christians believe that:

> *God chose what is foolish in the world . . .*
> *God chose what is weak in the world . . .*
> *God chose what is low and despised in the*
> *world . . . (1 Cor. 1:27-29).*

It is not therefore necessarily Christian to believe that God in choosing the foolish and weak and low and despised transformed them into the wise, the mighty, the high and the respected in the land. They could remain exactly what they are and still serve the divine purpose. This is true of the authors of our Gospels; it is true of the twenty centuries of interpretation that followed them. It is ultimately our faith that discerns the word of God in what they say. Only faith opens our eyes to the divine element both in Scripture and tradition.

Those Gospels are the word of God for me today because my faith and the faith of the community to which I belong accepts them as canonical Scriptures. They come to us as expressions of faith in Jesus Christ by four individuals writing for their communities some two thousand years ago. They come to us refracted through centuries of tradition which our church preserves and cherishes. We know that all this is human interpretation subject to all the limitations of the human condition. But we also believe that the same Holy Spirit is ever present, inspiring, directing, guiding, teaching and bringing to "remembrance all that I have said to you" (Jn. 14:26).

What gives the Scriptures their unending life is their ability to challenge Christians to respond to the person of Jesus Christ. Each Gospel is a different and unique understanding of the implications of that challenge. There is no one uniform and monolithic response to any one of them individually or to all of them collectively. Truths are eternal only in their ability to be resurrected to successive new lives by those who question them and are in turn questioned by them. They are eternal not by the new interpretations they inspire but by the newness of life they generate in response to their challenge.

In dealing with each Gospel, an attempt was made to illustrate different methods of interpretation and to show a variety of possible approaches. Naturally enough, no one method is fully adequate; no one interpretation is final and definitive. These Gospels are the word of God to us because they constantly challenge us to respond to:

"What do you think of the Christ?"

In the responses they themselves furnish to this question, the Gospels are a constant reminder to us that the acceptance of the challenge is not a creed confessed but a life lived. That life is unique and individual to each believer. It is the only proof anybody, Christian or non-Christian, possesses that this believer really believes the Gospels to be the word of God. In Christianity the life of the believer is the only valid and acceptable demonstration of the word of God in our Gospels.

Bibliography

For the questions of inspiration and the canon see:

Richard F. Smith, "Inspiration and Inerrancy," in the *Jerome Biblical Commentary* (Englewood Cliffs, N.J.: Prentice-Hall, 1968), pp. 499-514.

James C. Turro and Raymond E. Brown, "Canonicity," in *Jerome Biblical Commentary,* pp. 515-534.

Lionel Swain, "Inspiration of the Bible," in *A New Catholic Commentary on Holy Scripture* (Camden, N.J.: Thomas Nelson, 1969), pp. 53-60.

R. C. Fuller and R. J. Foster, "The Formation of the Canon," in *New Catholic Commentary,* pp. 21-31.

Gerhard Lohfink, *The Gospels: God's Word in Human Words,* Herald Biblical Booklets (Chicago, Ill.: Franciscan Herald Press, 1972).

For the development of New Testament interpretation in recent times see:

Stephen Neill, *The Interpretation of the New Testament 1861-1961* (New York: Oxford University Press, 1966);

or one of the following introductions to the New Testament:

W. D. Davies, *Invitation to the New Testament* (Garden City, N.Y.: Doubleday Anchor Books, 1969).

A. M. Hunter, *Introducing the New Testament,* 3rd revised edition (Philadelphia, Pa.: Westminister Press, 1972).

Pheme Perkins, *Reading the New Testament. An Introduction* (New York, N.Y.: Paulist Press, 1977).

Norman Perrin, *The New Testament. An Introduction* (New York, N.Y.: Harcourt Brace Jovanovich, 1974).

For the study of the Synoptic Gospels the following synopsis is most useful:
Burton H. Throckmorton, Jr., ed., *Gospel Parallels. A Synopsis of the First Three Gospels* (New York, N.Y.: Thomas Nelson, 1973).

For the individual Gospels see in "Herald Biblical Booklets" (Chicago, Ill.: Franciscan Press):
Robert J. Karris, *Following Jesus: A Guide to the Gospels.*
Donald Senior, *Matthew: A Gospel for the Church.*
Ludger Schenke, *Glory and the Way of the Cross. Gospel of Mark.*
George W. MacRae, *Faith in the Word: The Fourth Gospel.*

A very useful and handy series of commentaries on the individual Gospels is The Pelican Gospel Commentaries (Penguin Books):
J. C. Fenton, *Saint Matthew.*
D. E. Nineham, *Saint Mark.*
G. B. Caird, *Saint Luke.*
John Marsh, *Saint John.*

Index to New Testament References